“The O[illegible] [illegible]nd Organs o[illegible] [illegible]e Welsh Cathedrals in the 20th Century”

Compiled by Enid Bird

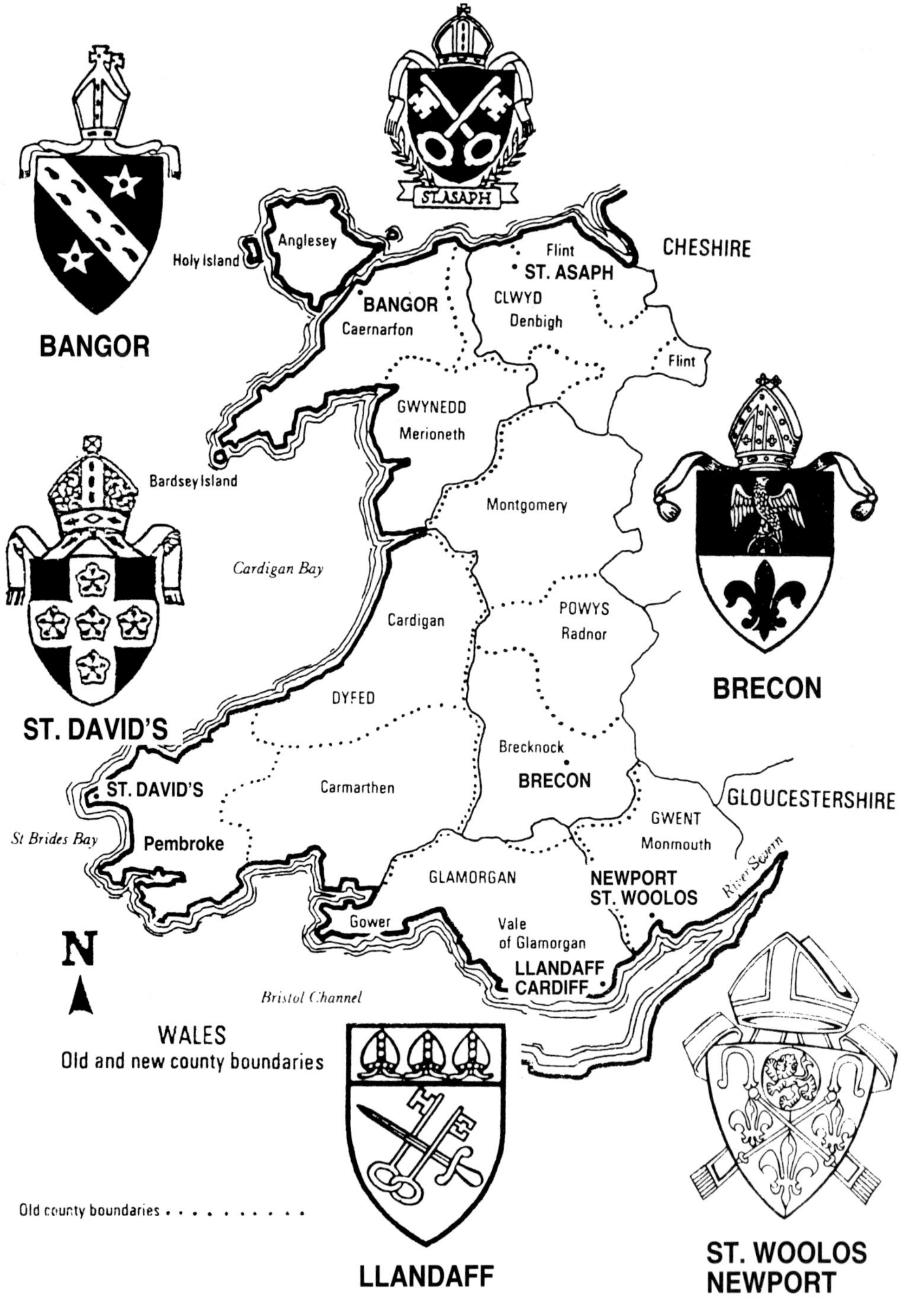

BANGOR
ST. ASAPH
ST. DAVID'S
BRECON
LLANDAFF
ST. WOOLOS
NEWPORT
Anglesey
Holy Island
BANGOR
Caernarfon
Flint
ST. ASAPH
CLWYD
Denbigh
CHESHIRE
Flint
GWYNEDD
Merioneth
Bardsey Island
Montgomery
Cardigan Bay
Cardigan
POWYS
Radnor
DYFED
Brecknock
BRECON
Carmarthen
ST. DAVID'S
St Brides Bay
Pembroke
GLOUCESTERSHIRE
GWENT
Monmouth
GLAMORGAN
NEWPORT
ST. WOOLOS
River Severn
Gower
Vale of Glamorgan
LLANDAFF
CARDIFF
Bristol Channel
N
WALES
Old and new county boundaries
Old county boundaries

ACKNOWLEDGEMENTS

The Organists and Masters of the Choristers of the six Welsh Cathedrals have given me valuable assistance in the compilation of this book in providing information and photographs. I am very much indebted to them in particular, and I also wish to thank the following people for their help:-

BATE, D. W., F.R.C.O., L.R.A.M., L.T.C.L. Cardiff.

BELCHER, J. T., M.A., F.R.C.O.(CHM), A.R.C.M. Organist and Master of the Choristers, Tewkesbury Abbey.

BOORMAN, Peter, Haverfordwest.

BUTCHER, A. V., M.A., D.Mus., F.R.C.O., Worcester.

CARDEN, Michael, Brecon, for photograph of J. Humphrey Carden.

COUSINS, M. E., F.R.C.O.(CHM), Organist of Mansfield Parish Church, Notts., for loan of photograph of C. K. Turner.

DAVIES, D. G., B.A., Mus.B., Ph.D., F.R.C.O., L.R.A.M., Leicester.

DICKINSON, R. D., B.Mus., F.R.C.O.(CHM), L.R.A.M., Farnham, Surrey.

ELLIOT, G. J., M.A., Mus.B., Ph.D., F.R.C.O., Organist and Master of the Choristers, Chelmsford Cathedral.

FISHER, Roger M.A., F.R.C.O.(CHM), A.R.C.M., A.T.C.L., Organist and Master of the Choristers, Chester Cathedral, for photograph of J. R. Middleton.

FLETCHER, E. H., M.A., Mus.B., F.R.C.O., Sanderstead, Surrey.

GABB, W. H., C.V.O., Mus.D., F.R.C.O., A.R.C.M., Chobham Parish Church, Surrey.

GRIMSBY TEAM MINISTRY, Parish Church of St. James, for photograph of E. A. Coningsby.

HAMPSON, Desmond, Solva, Pembrokeshire.

HESFORD, M. B., D.Mus., M.A., A.R.C.M., L.R.A.M., Organist, Collegiate Church of St. Nicholas, Galway, Eire.

HYWELL, John, M.Mus., A.R.C.O., Music Department, University of Wales, Bangor.

JACKSON, Sir Nicholas, B.T., L.R.A.M., A.R.C.M., London.

JAMES, Nevil, Archivist, Llandaff Cathedral.

JOYCE, R. H., M.A., Mus.B., F.R.C.O., Senior Lecturer at Welsh College of Music and Drama, Cardiff.

LAMB, Andrew, Organ Scholar, St. David's Cathedral.

MIDDLETON DR, G. W., St. David's.

PAUL, Mrs G., Bangor, for photograph of her late husband.

PRICE, D. R., Bangor.

RANDLE, A., Director of Music, Arnold Lodge School, Leamington Spa.

REES, Nona, Hon. Sub-Librarian, St. David's Cathedral.

SMITH, P. A., Assistant Organist, St. Asaph Cathedral.

WATTS, M. G., B.Mus., Dip.Ed., Cardigan.

"The Organists and Organs of the Welsh Cathedrals in the 20th Century"

List of names of the Organists of the Welsh Cathedrals

BALL, Cyril James 1905-75	St. Woolos Cathedral
BARTON, Christopher Michael John – born 1956	St. Woolos Cathedral
BATE, Donald William – born 1912	St. Woolos Cathedral
BEALE, George Galloway – 1868-1936	Llandaff Cathedral
BEAUMONT, Kerry Jason – born 1957	St. David's Cathedral
BELCHER, John Theodore – born 1937	St. Asaph Cathedral
BELCHER, William Edward – 1864-	St. Asaph Cathedral
BOORMAN, Peter – born 1923	St. David's Cathedral
BUTCHER, Albert Vernon – born 1909	Llandaff Cathedral
CARDEN, John Humphrey – 1886-1957	Brecon Cathedral
CONINGSBY, Eric Alfred – 1909-55	Llandaff Cathedral
DAVIES, David Gwerfyl – born 1913	Brecon Cathedral
DAVIES, Hugh H. – born 1952	St. Asaph Cathedral
DICKINSON, Robert Duke – born 1916	St. Asaph Cathedral
ELLIOTT, Graham John – born 1947	St. Asaph Cathedral
FLETCHER, Eric Howard – born 1933	Llandaff Cathedral
GABB, William Henry – born 1909	Llandaff Cathedral
GACCON, John Augustus – 1869-1934	St. Woolos Cathedral
GEDGE, David Patrick – born 1939	Brecon Cathedral
GOODWIN, Andrew John – born 1947	Bangor Cathedral
HALLFORD, Thomas – 1911-50	Llandaff Cathedral
HESFORD, Michael Bryan – born 1930	Brecon Cathedral
HYWEL, John – born 1941	Bangor Cathedral
JACKSON, Nicholas – born 1934	St. David's Cathedral
JOHN'S, Charles St. Ervan – 1896-1963	St. Woolos Cathedral
JOYCE, Robert Henry – born 1927	Llandaff Cathedral
MORGAN, Thomas Westlake – 1869	Bangor Cathedral
MORRIS, Herbert Charles – 1873-1940	St. David's Cathedral
MIDDLETON, James Roland – 1896-1983	St. Asaph Cathedral
PAUL, Leslie Douglas – 1903-69	Bangor Cathedral
ROGERS, Roland – 1847-1927	Bangor Cathedral
ROOTHAM, Cyril Bradley – 1875-1938	St. Asaph Cathedral
SMITH, Michael John – born 1937	Llandaff Cathedral
SOAR, Joseph – 1878-1971	St. David's Cathedral
STOCKS, Harold Carpenter Lumb – 1884-1956	St. Asaph Cathedral
TURNER, Charles Kenneth – 1904-59	Llandaff Cathedral
WATTS, Malcolm Gruffydd – born 1947	St. David's Cathedral
WILSON, Archibald Wayet(t) – 1869-1950	St. Asaph Cathedral

BANGOR CATHEDRAL
EGLWYS GADEIROL BANGOR

* Bangor Cathedral stands on one of the oldest ecclesiastical sites in Britain, having been founded in the 6th Century, c525, even before Augustine established the See of Canterbury. Deniol, the founder of the See, was consecrated bishop, c. 546, some 20 years later.

*** BANGOR CATHEDRAL ORGANISTS**

Thomas Westlake Morgan	1892-1906
Roland Rogers	1906-1927 re-appointed
Leslie Douglas Paul	1928-1969
John Hywel	1970-1971
Andrew John Goodwin	1972

ROLAND ROGERS was born at West Bromwich on 17th November, 1847.

He received his early musical training from his father. He was appointed to play the organ at St. Peter's Church, West Bromwich in 1858 at the age of 11, at St. John's Church, Wolverhampton in 1862 and then at Tettenhall Parish Church in 1867. He took the degree of B.Mus. in 1870, becoming organist of Bangor Cathedral in 1871. He proceeded to the D.Mus. degree in 1875, both degrees being from Oxford University.

Rogers left Bangor Cathedral in 1892 because of the strained relationship between himself and the Dean brought about because he was conducting musical performances in nonconformist chapels. His resignation was accepted "with deep regret". The Vicar of Bangor, however, appointed him as organist of the Parish Church of St. James until he resumed his former post as organist of the Cathedral in 1906, and held it until his death on 30th July, 1927.

He was a well-known organist and was called upon to superintend the setting up of organs in numerous churches and chapels and to give inaugural recitals on them. He did excellent work as a teacher and was Instructor of Music at Bangor University College and at the Royal Mount School, Colwyn Bay.

A Bethesda Choir won the prize at three National eisteddfodau under his direction – at Denbigh, 1882, Cardiff, 1883, and Liverpool, 1884. He also adjudicated at the Bangor National Eisteddfod of 1874. He took the prize at the Llandudno National Eisteddfod for a Cantata, "The Garden". He wrote other cantatas – "Out of the Deep", "Prayer and Praise", which work is quoted on the inscription in Bangor Cathedral, but obviously quoted wrongly as it is musically incorrect. The inscription reads:

To the Glory of God and in memory of
ROLAND ROGERS,
DOCTOR OF MUSIC
A great organist and conductor of choirs.
Also a talented composer, who gave of his best to the service of GOD, in this cathedral for forty-one years.
Entered into rest July 30th, 1927 aged 80.

Servant well done.
"Prayer and Praise", Rogers Mus. Doc.

Another cantata was "Floribel", and he also wrote church music, anthems and part-songs "The river gloweth strong", and "Y Storm" which gained much popularity. He edited the Welsh Psalter and was conductor of the Welsh Choral Society. Recollections by him appeared in the North Wales Chronicle of November and December, 1926.

Although he came back to the cathedral for a second term of office in 1906, as Dr. Leslie Paul says 'Rogers appeared to be an embittered and disillusioned man in his later years. In straitened circumstances he worked hard until his eightieth year, when his health finally failed'. Dr. Paul remembers him, short in stature but impressive in appearance, until the end wearing top hat and frock-coat for all cathedral services. Rogers made tours as a recitalist. Dr. Paul compiled a chant book for use at Bangor, and he says that there were some very good chants by Dr. Rogers included in the book.

He was buried in Glanadda cemetery, Bangor. Although the inscription in Bangor Cathedral says that he was 80, he died at the age of 79.

THOMAS WESTLAKE MORGAN was born on 6th August, 1869 at Congresbury, near Weston-super-Mare, Somerset. He became a chorister at King's College, Cambridge, and afterwards a pupil of Dorchester Grammar School and then Pupil-Assistant at King's College to Dr. Mann. Previous to this he was a pupil of Mr Boynton Smith in 1883 and two years later was organist of St. Catharine's College, Cambridge, 1885.

From here he went to Paris as organist of St. George's Anglican Church remaining a year and returning to London to enter the Royal College of Music where he studied with Sir Walter Parratt and Dr. F. E. Gladstone. He was organist of St. John's Church, Wilton Road, London in 1890, and in 1891, went to St. David's Church, Merthyr Tydfil where he was also conductor of the Merthyr Philharmonic Society.

In 1892 he was appointed Organist of Bangor Cathedral and while there was also choir-master at St. Paul's Church, Colwyn Bay and at Conwy Parish Church and was given a bardic title at the Gorsedd in 1901. He was Music Master (Professor of Music) at the North Wales Training College, Bangor from 1895-7. In 1892 he became Vice-President and Hon. Fellow of the Guild of Organists, and in 1894, Examiner to the Incorporated Society of Musicians. He was the founder and Hon. Secretary of the Welsh Section of the Incorporated Society of Professional Musicians.

To quote from Dr. Leslie Paul, "Music at Bangor Cathedral Church, Some Historical Notes", Tom Westlake Morgan was a hard task-master, insisting on practices for the boys before they went to school each morning, and in 1892, for the first time, there were daily choral services for the four summer months from June to September. It is not surprising that results were achieved.

In 1895, the bi-centenary of Purcell's death was commemorated in London, and the Bangor choir was invited to take part in the special service in Westminster Abbey. Later, the choir entertained royalty in Penrhyn Castle. Westlake Morgan was also responsible for the superlative organ built by Hill in 1897. It was opened with a recital by Sir Walter Parratt, organist of St. George's Chapel, Windsor, in 1897.

This instrument incorporated the best of the earlier organ, but was a much more ambitious project, with a fourth (solo) manual and two genuine 32′ pedal stops. It was an instrument of pedigree and beautiful quality, but was handicapped by its site. No doubt the Dean and Chapter wished to keep the north transept clear, and the whole of this large organ – apart from the 32′ stops and 16′ open metal – was crammed into the chamber, which was hardly large enough for the previous three-manual organ. Tubas were double-mitred, and the pedal organ in particular was stifled.

This organ had great character, but was again too distant for any big congregational services.

Westlake Morgan was the composer and editor of church music also and he gave many organ recitals and was reputed to be a fine musician. He left Bangor in 1906 and in the latter part of 1907 became organist of St. Bride's Church, Fleet Street.

His whereabouts after this are uncertain, but an article published in "Musical Opinion", February 1969, states that: "Dr. T. Westlake Morgan was appointed organist of the Futurist Cinema, Scarborough, shortly after its formal opening which took place on Sunday, September 4th, 1921. Horace Shepherd, Mus. Bac., gave the opening recital." It states also that "Dr. T. Westlake Morgan had given a series of Sunday concerts at the Royal Albert Hall, and he had toured the continent and USA. In 1920 he had toured the music halls with the Hill, Norman and Beard organ built for Major Harvey Bathurst."

A photograph of Thomas Westlake Morgan is to be found in 'Notable Welsh Musicians" edited by Frederick Griffiths, 1896. Dr. Paul says that he is best remembered for the magnificent way in which he raised the choir at Bangor Cathedral to a peak of excellence hitherto unreached. According to the 1937 'Who's Who in Music', he was living in London at that time.

LESLIE DOUGLAS PAUL was born on 8th March, 1903 in Bangor. He received his musical training at Clifton College, Bristol (as a music scholar), from 1918-21. He went on to the Royal Academy of Music (where he won an open organ scholarship), and then to Keble College, Oxford, in 1922, graduating M.A. in 1929 having gained the B.Mus. in 1927.

His first appointment was as assistant music master at Winchester College from 1924-6 and at Warriston School, Moffat, Dumfries from 1926, after which he returned to Bangor in 1927 as organist of the cathedral being at this time, the youngest cathedral organist in Britain,

In 1941, he served with the R.A.F., and after 4 years' absence, returned to Bangor Cathedral and continued to maintain the choral tradition at Bangor for some 40 years; which was difficult as there was no choir school, and choristers had to be recruited from local schools. He was an excellent and caring teacher both of organ, piano and academic skills.

He had many notable pupils and choristers – most famous of whom is Dr. George Guest who recently retired after being the Organist of St. John's College, Cambridge; also Arnold Lewis, a former Head of Music, B.B.C. Wales, Richard Elfyn Jones (lecturer, Music Department, University of Cardiff and former conductor of the Cardiff Polyphonic Choir), Carys Hughes, organ recitalist and John Hywel who followed Dr. Paul.

In 1951, Leslie Paul was awarded the Executants degree of D.Mus., by the University of Edinburgh and at other times he was elected a Fellow of the Royal Academy of Music and the Royal College of Organists, and became A.R.C.M.

Dr. Paul had other musical interests. He successfully toured India in 1946, New Zealand in 1948, and West Indies in 1957 as an examiner and recitalist and he broadcast from seven different countries. He was well known as an adjudicator of leading music festivals, and had published compositions including 'Praise of Earth', a song cycle of Elizabethan lyrics, a setting of the Evening Service in D, school songs and other pianoforte music and church music.

His special studies were organ recitals, and pianoforte and singing tuition. He wrote various articles in periodicals, one of these being an article on the Music at Bangor Cathedral Church: some Historical Notes published in 'Welsh Music' (Spring 1971).

From 1954, he was an Examiner for the Associated Board of the Royal Schools of Music and he was a member of the Music Advisory Board, 1958-60. He was Special Commissioner for the Royal School of Church Music from 1960, and was an External Assessor for the B.B.C. Auditions (Welsh Home Service). He was North Wales Hon. Member of the Music Advisory Board, R.S.C.M. and was local representative of the Incorporated Society of Musicians and the Royal Academy of Music.

He founded the Bangor Organ Club, both to attract some of the world's finest executants to the magnificent instrument at Bangor Cathedral (including Jeanne Demessieux), and to give his students and fellow members of the society the opportunity of performing on good organs in North Wales churches. A kind and understanding man he died tragically in the year following his retirement on 12th October, 1970 and the inscription in Bangor Cathedral reads;-

In memory of
LESLIE PAUL, D.MUS.,F.R.C.O.,F.R.A.M.
Organist and Master of the Choristers, 1927-1969.
Given by friends and former choristers.

JOHN HYWELL was Director of Music at Bangor Cathedral from January 1970 to July 1971.

He was born in Cemaes Bay, Anglesey in 1941, and was educated at Sir Thomas Jones Comprehensive School, Amlwch from 1951-59, going on to the University College of North Wales, Bangor from 1959-64, where he gained a B.Mus. Honours degree in 1962 and an M.Mus. degree in 1964.

Whilest he was at the University, he studied the organ with Dr. Leslie Paul, organist of Bangor Cathedral gaining the A.R.C.O. diploma. During 1964-65, he attended the Royal Academy of Music in London, pursuing courses in conducting, composition, piano and 'cello. In July 1965 he was awarded the Ernest Read Prize for the Outstanding Conductor of the Year. He was Head of Music at the Oadby Beauchamp Grammar School, Oadby, Leicester from 1965-66.

In 1966 he was appointed Assistant Lecturer in Music at the University College of North Wales, Bangor, becoming a full Lecturer in 1967. In 1979 he was promoted to Senior Lecturer, and was Acting Head of Department from 1987-88 when Professor Mathias took early retirement, becoming during his last nine months Head of Department for the period October 1988 to July 1991.

At Bangor Cathedral he chose all the music and trained and conducted the Choir, while William Bacon (Organist at Beaumaris Parish Church) played the organ under his supervision. He, with the Dean, appointed Andrew Goodwin, a Liverpool University B.A. graduate as the first organ scholar, to work under the direction of John Hywel, and he succeeded W. Bacon as organist in October 1970, whilst reading for his M.A., at Bangor University.

During Hywel's term of office he expanded the scope and activities of the Choir, and added several services and anthems to the repertoire and increased the public perception of the choir by taking it out of the Cathedral to sing in some of the major churches in the Diocese. The choir also sang Nine Lessons and Carols (entirely in Welsh) for BBC TV Wales which was transmitted on Christmas Day, 1970. He resigned in July 1971 because of pressure of work.

John Hywel has many compositions to his name and his special study is conducting choirs. His recreation is mountain walking, travelling, and wining and dining.

ANDREW JOHN GOODWIN was born at Hillingdon, Middlesex in 1947. He was educated at Wolverhampton Grammar School and afterwards at the University of Liverpool where he read for an honours degree in Music. Whilst at Liverpool, he studied the Organ with the late Dr. Caleb Jarvis who was Organist of St. George's Hall for many years.

In 1970, Andrew Goodwin became Organ Scholar at Bangor Cathedral and a postgraduate student at the University College of North Wales where he carried out research culminating in an M.A. thesis on 'The Anthems of Maurice Green'.

In 1972, Andrew Goodwin was appointed Organist and Master of the Choristers at Bangor, probably Britain's oldest Cathedral foundation. Since that time, he has extensively developed the role and repertoire of the Cathedral Choir.

His frequent travels with the Choir have included a tour to Germany in 1983. Over the years, he has been involved with a number of broadcasts and recordings from Bangor, both with the Choir and as an organ soloist.

Andrew Goodwin is involved in many musical activities outside the Cathedral, as a recitalist, conductor and a teacher. He is part-time Tutor in Organ at the University in Bangor and an examiner to the Associated Board of the Royal Schools of Music.

He is very interested in Wildlife Conservation and in the Theatre. However, his principal extra-musical concern is with railways. Since 1986 he has been very much involved with British Rail and its customer relations.

At the time of writing, he is chairman of two customer consultation bodies for North-West England, North and Mid Wales; he has also acted as a consultant lecturer to B.R. management and staff.

BANGOR CATHEDRAL ORGAN

The following extract is taken from 'Cathedral Organists, Past and Present', by John E. West and published by Novello & Co., Ltd, London:- 'From the following it appears that there must have been an organist at Bangor Cathedral as early as 1360, if not before:- 'The celebrated Bard, Dafydd ab Gwilym, who wrote in the fourteenth century, makes particular mention of an organ and choir at Bangor in his time, in a commendatory Ode addressed to Hywel, Dean of Bangor in his time, which was in Welsh, has the following: "Whose organ, and harmonious choir are unrivalled in performance".

Hywel was made Dean of Bangor in 1359 and Bishop in 1370. This Ode, therefore, must have been written between 1359 and 1370, and the allusion to an organ renders it obvious there must have been an Organist at that time'.

William Hill installed a 3 manual organ in 1873, replacing a 3 manual Samuel Green organ of 1779. The 1873 organ was enlarged to 4 manuals in 1897.

The following extract was supplied by Andrew Goodwin.

The organ was completely re-planned and reconstructed in 1954 by The John Compton Organ Company, Ltd., of London. The Great, Swell and Pedal organs have been brought out of the organ chamber and re-erected in the North Transept where their tone will be unobstructed and access for tuning greatly improved.

The Solo Organ now speaks through the Western Arch of the organ chamber, the Choir Organ through the South West Arch, and the entirely new and beautiful console is detached and placed in the South Transept so that the organist can hear the organ, choir and congregation in proper proportion.

The action throughout is electro-pneumatic of the most modern type. The rebuilding of the organ has provided the opportunity of completing the tonal scheme and the organ now contains 85 speaking registers and 22 couplers, making a total of 107 stopknobs. All the pistons are adjustable at the Console. The manual keys are covered with finest ivory of ⅓″ thickness, and their compass is now 61 notes. The pedalboard is of 32 notes and of concave and radiating pattern. Wind pressures in the organ range from 2½″ to 15″ and a new blowing apparatus has been installed (the organ contains 4,210 pipes).

In 1987, a four year appeal was launched to raise £300,000, part of which is for essential work on the organ, one of the finest in the Principality.

MUSIC AT BANGOR CATHEDRAL

Andrew Goodwin was appointed Organist of the Cathedral in 1972. His priorities for the music of the Cathedral have been to achieve a standard of excellence in a widely varied repertoire, to ensure that as many as possible have the opportunity of participating in performance and to make cathedral music available to the widest possible audience.

The Cathedral has no choir school; boys are drawn from a wide area. Parental support is therefore crucial, and recent years have seen the formation and growth of a flourishing Choir Association. As well as two choral services on Sundays there are choral evensongs for boys' voices on Tuesdays and for full choir on Thursdays. In addition the Choir frequently sings at services of other churches in the diocese.

Regular concerts are given by the Choir and a recent tour of Germany iuncluded performances in Mannheim and in Worms Cathedral. The Choir gave the first performance of William Mathias's anthem "Hear, O thou shepherd of Israel" in 1983, a work commissioned for the Enthronement service for the Bishop of Bangor. The Choir has recently sung at St. Paul's Cathedral and at the Royal Albert Hall.

Closer links with the University College of North Wales, Bangor ensure that the Cathedral is able to obtain organ scholars; lay clerks are sometimes drawn from University staff and students.

Regular recitals are given on the Cathedral's fine four-manual Hill organ. Andrew Goodwin gives some of these recitals as well as touring extensively to perform at many venues. His particular interest is the music of Franck. He also places emphasis on the art of extemporisation.

Elizabeth Le Grove
North-East Worcestershire College, Bromsgrove.

BRECON CATHEDRAL

The new diocese of Swansea and Brecon came into being on St. John's Day, 1923, whereupon St. John's Priory Church became the Cathedral.

BRECON CATHEDRAL ORGANISTS

John Humphrey Carden	1923-1956	Michael Bryan Hesford	1963-1966
David Gwerfyl Davies	1956-1962	David Patrick Gedge	1966

JOHN HUMPHREY CARDEN was born at Row, Dunbartonshire on 21st June, 1886. He was educated at Hereford Cathedral where he was a chorister and was articled to Dr. G. R. Sinclair, the Cathedral Organist and his successor, Percy Hull. He was Organist of St. Peter's Church, Hereford from 1920-23, and prior to this at St. Peter's, Glasbury-on-Wye from 1907-12. He was appointed to Brecon Cathedral in 1923 as the first Cathedral organist and here he remained until 1956, when he retired. He died on 21st September, 1957 at Brecon.

To quote from 'Music at Brecon Cathedral', by David Gedge, 'Daily Choral Evensong was established during the time of Humphrey Carden, sung by treble voices only with the result that canticles were sung to chants and there were no anthems. Apparently, discipline at practices was strict, especially with regard to attendance'.

DAVID GWERFYL DAVIES was born at Dowlais, Merthyr Tydfil, Wales on 1st February, 1913 and was educated at Merthyr Tydfil County Grammar School and at the University College, Cardiff from 1932-7, where he read music and took the B.A. degree. He later took the Mus.B. at Trinity College, Dublin. He is also the holder of the F.R.C.O. and L.R.A.M. diplomas and is Ph.D.

He left the R.A.F. in 1946 and took up an appointment as Music Master at Alderman Newton's Boys' School, Leicester. Subsequent appointments were at Bromsgrove, Merthyr Tydfil and in 1958 he became Organist at Brecon Cathedral.

Davies took up his appointment on Whit-Sunday having been Music Master at Cyfarthfa Castle Grammar School, Merthyr Tydfil and Organist and Choirmaster of St. John's Church, Dowlais. He took on also the post of Music Master at Brecon Boys' Grammar School yet he found time to initiate a series of organ recitals after Evensong on Sundays. He also organised a special service sung by the combined choirs of the Cathedral and Christ College, with those of St. David's and St. Mary's Churches, Brecon, which took place on the Festival of St. Luke the Evangelist, October 18th, 1958.

He remained at Brecon Cathedral until 1963 when he moved to Leicester as Music Adviser to the Leicester Education Committee which post he retained until 1980. He was also the Organist and Choirmaster at St. Peter's Church, Highfields.

Dr. Davies formed the City of Leicester Singers soon after his arrival in Leicester and was its Director of Music until 1989. The Choir performed a wide range of music during his tenure. He was an Examiner to Trinity College of Music, London from 1968.

Dr. Davies now has plenty of time to enjoy travelling, listening to music and playing a little golf.

MICHAEL BRYAN HESFORD was born at Eccles, Manchester on 19th July, 1930. He received his education at William Hulme's Grammar School, Manchester, and studied music and the organ with W. H. Selby at St. Peter's Church, Stockport, and later with William Hardwick at St. Ann's, Manchester, and also with Caleb Jarvis of Liverpool. At the instigation of, and recommended by Henry Willis III he undertook lessons under Marcel Dupré in Paris. At the same time he had a few lessons with Jean Langlais whilst also studying in Germany under Max Drischner.

His main appointments as Organist and Choirmaster have been:- Assistant Organist of St. Peter's Church, Stockport, 1950-52, Organist and Choirmaster of Glossop Parish Church, 1953-55, Organist and Choirmaster of Northenden Parish Church, 1955, also Organist and Choirmaster of St. Philip's Church, Gorton, Manchester, 1955-56.

From 1956-59 he was Organist and Choirmaster of Prescot Parish Church and Music Master of Knowsley Woolfall Secondary School. An appointment as Assistant Organist of Newcastle Cathedral from 1959-60 came next and then he went to Wymondham Abbey from 1960-63 when he was also Music Master of Wymondham Boys' School.

His next appointment was to Brecon Cathedral as Organist and Master of the Choristers in 1963. He left in mid-January 1966 and was succeeded by David Gedge at Easter that year.

Bryan Hesford went on to the Priory and Parish Church of St. Margaret's King's Lynn from 1966-70 and from 1970-71 he was Organist of Lancaster Priory. From 1971-73 he was Organist at St. Barnabas, Tunbridge Wells and from 1973-78 he was at Melton Mowbray Parish Church. In 1985 he went to Norway as Organist of Skånevik and Etne and his current appointment is at the Collegiate (and pro cathedral) Church of St. Nicholas, Galway, Eire.

In addition to his organist's duties, Bryan Hesford was Senior Examiner at the Trinity College of Music, London from 1967-85 also he was Editor of the Musical Opinion from 1976-85 and Editor of The Organ from 1976-80.

As a composer, his work has centred on the Anglican Liturgy with settings (ASB) for the Collegiate Church of St. Nicholas, Galway, Newcastle Cathedral and Killala Cathedral. Other liturgical works include a Mass (in Hungarian) for Eger Cathedral, and a Requiem Mass for the Kiev Philharmonic Society, a Magnificat and Nunc Dimittis for Newcastle Cathedral and Leicester Cathedral also organ works for Berlin Cathedral, Rottenbuch Abbey and Riga Dom (Latvia).

As a recitalist he has played at many venues:- St. Paul's Cathedral, Westminster Abbey, Rochester Cathedral, St. Mary's Cathedral Edinburgh, Norwich Cathedral, St. David's Cathedral, Brecon Cathedral, Newcastle Cathedral and Wells Cathedral.

He has played also at King's College and St. John's College, Cambridge and abroad at Bach-Kirche, Arnstadt, Meissen Cathedral, Hofkirche Dresden, Riga, Vilnius, Tallin, Leningrad, Moscow, Kiev, Kishinev, Norosibirsk, Bohosudov (Czechoslovakia), Trondheim Cathedral, Breslau, Ottobeuren, Berlin, Rostock, Greifswald, Notre Dame de Paris.

He has made a recording for Melodia (USSR) on the organ of Riga Dom. His qualifications are:- D.Mus. of the Geneva Theological College, USA, Ph.D., M.A., A.R.C.M., L.R.A.M.

DAVID PATRICK GEDGE was born on 12th March, 1939 in London. He was educated at St. Olave's Grammar School from 1947-57 and was also a chorister (treble, then alto and bass) at Southwark Cathedral from 1947-62. David Gedge sang the part of the boy Nicholas in the first London performance of Benjamin Britten's St. Nicolas and also sang in the choir at the Coro-nation of Queen Elizabeth II on 2nd June, 1953. David Gedge's father, Vicar of Holy Trinity Church, Lambeth, was immortalised as Mr Gedge, the clergyman in Benjamin Britten's opera, 'Albert Herring'.*

* Opera Magazine, May 1992, Vol. 43 No. 5.

He became a Junior Exhibitioner at the Royal Academy of Music (1952-57) and played the viola in the London Junior Orchestra and the London Schools Symphony Orchestra. He was Assistant Organist at St. Stephen's Church, South Dulwich, London (1955-57) and Organist and Choirmaster at St. Mary the Virgin, Primrose Hill, London NW3 (1957-62).

During this time he was (1956-62), Conductor of the Thomas Morley Chamber Orchestra. Whilst at the Royal Academy of Music where he studied from (1957-62) he studied the organ with C. H. Trevor and viola with Max Gilbert and Winifred Copperwheat gaining the L.R.A.M. in 1959, the G.R.S.M. in 1960 and the F.R.C.O. in 1962 winning the Turpin Prize. He was awarded the A.R.A.M. in 1977.

He next proceeded to the Institute of Education at London University from 1960-61 gaining the Dip.Ed. in 1962 whereupon he became Organist and Choirmaster of Selby Abbey, 1962-66, and Founder and Conductor of the Selby Choral Society, 1963-66, and Founder-Chairman of Selby Music Club, 1963-6, also Founder-Chairman of Selby Festival, 1965. He was Music Master of Howden County Secondary School, 1963-64 and Head of the Music Department, Selby High School, 1964-66.

He then moved to Wales to be Organist of Brecon Cathedral and St. Mary's Church, Brecon and he has also been Head of the Music Department, Buith Wells High School since 1966. He is the Founder and Conductor of the Cathedral Singers from 1966, and in 1975 he formed also the Gwent Chamber Orchestra.

He has given lectures for the W.E.A. and for the University College, Cardiff, Extra Mural Department and has had articles on 19th Century Cathedral Musicians etc., published in Cotswold Life, County Life, Country Quest, Musical Opinion, Musical Times, Times Educational Supplement, The Organ and also The Western Mail.

Hazel Davies, wife of David Gedge, who was born in Cydweli, Dyfed, and was also a pupil of C. H. Trevor at the Royal Academy of Music, is Assistant Organist at Brecon Cathedral.

BRECON CATHEDRAL ORGAN

– The following account is taken from "Music at Brecon Cathedral", by David Gedge, Organist and Choirmaster at Brecon Cathedral.

In 'Cathedrals, Abbeys and Churches' edited by Professor T. G. Bonney, Hon. Canon of Manchester Cathedral, published towards the end of the nineteenth century, it is stated that the main organ in the Priory Church of St. John, Brecon at that time replaced an ancient instrument that originally came from Drury Lane Theatre, London, in 1789. However, in 'The Organ' magazine published in July 1934, the late Huskisson Stubington suggests that the present organ replaced an instrument which was brought to the Priory Church in 1877, from St. Mary's Church, Brecon. This old organ must be the one listed in the nineteenth century manuscript by a gentleman named Sperling; St. Mary's, Brecon or Brecknock built by Henry Holland in 1787, 2 rows of keys, Great organ GG long 8ves to F, swell to fiddle G.

When a new organ arrived at the Priory Church in 1886, the old instrument was given yet another home, supposedly at Clydach in the Swansea Valley. Presumably it is the organ referred to in the book by Professor Bonney.

The new organ was built by Messrs. William Hill and Son at a net cost of £1,100. The opening ceremonies took place on October 27th when Morning Service was followed by a public luncheon. Afterwards a recital was given by Dr. Langdon Colbourne, Organist of Hereford Cathedral, who played music by Felix Mendelssohn, Henry Smart, S. S. Wesley and Alexandre Guilmant.

At this time Thomas, elder son of the original William Hill, was in charge of the firm. As it was he who supervised the building or restoration of such famous organs as those at Beverley Minister, King's College, Cambridge, Ely and Lichfield Cathedrals, not surprisingly his instrument at Brecon was a tonal success. That it was not a success in other ways was due to the organ chamber being sited in a small, low-roofed chapel opening out of the South Transept.

This then was the organ installed for Rees Thomas Heins, Organist and Choirmaster at St. John's Priory Church, Brecon since 1879.

By 1927, the Cathedral organ at forty-one years of age, was in need of restoration. Unfortunately little money was available for this because so much had been used in restoring to the Cathedral both the precincts and the St. Lawrence Chapel that had long been a ruin. Although it was only possible to modernise the existing instrument, make a few tonal alterations and provide a mechanical blowing plant, nevertheless the opportunity was taken to move it into a chamber built specially above the former one.

Unfortunately it was practical only to provide an opening into the Chancel as any additional opening into the South Transept might have weakened the support of the central tower. Unfortunate also was the need to place the choir organ, far back in the new chamber because this prevented much of the sound from penetrating the building. The work was completed in 1931 when the removal of the mixture stop from the great organ was a sign of the times.

It was now possible for Humphrey Carden to establish a tradition of organ recitals in the Cathedral. He began with the best and brought George Cunningham, renowned Organist of Birmingham Town Hall to give the opening recital on the rebuilt instrument. Subsequent recitals included Percy Hull who had succeeded George Sinclair at Hereford Cathedral and George Thalben-Ball who had succeeded Walford Davies at the Temple Church, London.

Even during the Second World War these recitals continued and Harry Goss-Custard, Organist of Liverpool Cathedral, visited the Cathedral. Concerts were also given by the Cathedral Choir and by the Breconshire Orchestral Society, which was conducted by Humphrey Carden.

D. Gwerfyl Davies arrived as second Organist of Brecon. He initiated a series of organ recitals after Evensong on Sundays, and also he organised a special service sung by the combined choirs of the Cathedral and Christ College along with those of St. David's and St. Mary's Churches, Brecon which took place on the Festival of St. Luke the Evangelist, October 18th, 1958.

It did not take the new Cathedral Organist long to discover the problem that beset Humphrey Carden some twenty years before when the choir stalls had been moved from the Chancel to a position beneath the tower. Whenever the Organist sat at the console in the organ chamber to accompany the choir, he experienced considerable difficulty in hearing the singing. The remedy was obvious but expensive.

In 1962 the console was removed from this unfortunate position and placed in the North Transept behind the choir stalls (cantoris). The original organ case had been designed by W. D. Caroe when he was Cathedral Architect; now his son, A. D. R. Caroe added the screen beneath the case to cover the original site of the console.

Gwerfyl Davies did not long enjoy the luxury of hearing adequately both the organ and the choir because later that year he moved from Brecon to Leicester on becoming Music Adviser to the City of Leicester. His successor at the Cathedral, M. Bryan Hesford was at this time Organist and Choirmaster of Wymondham Abbey in Norfolk.

Perhaps the most exciting venture during David Gedge's period as Cathedral Organist as far as the organs are concerned has been the restoration of the old chamber organ standing in the south Transept of the Cathedral.

This was prompted by a decision of the Dean and Chapter to sell the instrument as scrap. Fortunately at the request of the Organist, Dean W. Ungoed Jacob, persuaded the Chapter to suspend this decision pending an enquiry into the state of the pipework. The London Organist, Robert Munns was called in to give a report on the organ and in preparing this, certain facts came to light.

It was known that the instrument had come from Hay Castle, and that it was referred to in the diaries of the Revd. Francis Kilvert. The organ had remained in Hay Castle until 1901, when Archdeacon W. L. Bevan, Vicar of Hay, had retired to Ely Tower, Brecon.

Presumably the organ was placed in store then because it is not thought that it was ever moved to Ely Tower. Certainly after 1907 it was moved to Pool House, Belmont Road, Hereford, the home of Mrs Mumford, grand-daughter of Archdeacon Bevan. Here it stood in the hall until 1923, when she moved to Weymouth.

This was the year when Edward Latham Bevan, son of Archdeacon Bevan, 'Teddy Bevan' of the Kilvert Diaries, became Bishop of Swansea and Brecon and it was he who had the organ brought to the Cathedral to be set up in the Corvizors Chapel. There it remained until 1963 when it was moved to allow for the completion of the screen around this chapel. It was then that some of the pipework was damaged.

An estimate for the complete restoration of the organ was submitted by Percy Daniel and Co. Ltd., Organ Builders of Clevedon, Avon. £800 was the sum required for the work and as this was forthcoming from the Kilvert Society, Friends of Brecon Cathedral and private donors, work was soon started.

So began a happy association between the firm of Percy Daniel and Co. Ltd., Managing Director, Walter Gulvin and the Cathedral Organist. When the organ was restored, it was mounted on castors and fitted with an electric blower but apart from these useful additions, it was left in its original condition. Certain oddities were retained, the octave of short toe pedals along with two 'combination' pedals and their respective cancellors, also the strangely-sited bellows at the top of the instrument.

As at some time an oboe stop had been substituted for another stop, probably a flute 4′, the opportunity was taken to reverse this. The new flute 4′ which fits into the tonal scheme ideally, is, in fact, from an instrument by J. J. Binns. The entire organ is enclosed but the shuttered front can be removed to render it unclosed.

A number of mysteries remain. Why does the organ casework belie the date 1789, which appears on the soundboard, yet this pre-dates, by five years the formation of Bevington and Sons, the firm from Greek Street, Soho, London, whose nameplate adorns the keyboard? The low G manual compass confirms that the instrument was built at around this time but does not the casework suggest that it was rebuilt some fifty or sixty years later, perhaps when the Revd. W. L. Bevan became Vicar of Hay?

Next year, on Holy Saturday, April 1st, 1972, the chamber organ was put to good use in a performance of J. S. Bach's St. John Passion. Shortly afterwards, Hazel Davies recorded for BBC Radio 3, the 'Twelve Short Pieces' which Samuel Wesley composed for such an organ.

One day during the following August, smoke was seen emitting from the main Cathedral Organ, giving a timely reminder that it was now forty-one years since the last major work was done. With 1973, the fiftieth anniversary of the Diocese and Bishop J. J. A. Thomas planning many special events at the Cathedral, something had to be done. In the Bishop the Organist had a good ally.

A scheme was drawn up with Percy Daniel and Co. Ltd., for the rebuilding and tonal remodelling of the organ, the price set at £11,580. Immediately the Bishop set about raising the money as one of the Acts of Thanksgiving to commemorate the Jubilee. Work was completed in time for Easter Day, April 22nd 1973, when the Archbishop of Wales preached at Choral Eucharist.

The redesigned organ was a great success, the scheme being drawn up by the Cathedral Organist and the Managing Director of Percy Daniel and Co. Ltd., along with many helpful suggestions from Kelvin Redford, a French Master at Christ College, who along with Hazel Davies had been acting as Assistant Organist.

David Gedge would like to complete the rebuild plans which he started in 1973 but that will cost £60,000 which for Brecon is a lot of money. However, 1993 is the 900th birthday of the Cathedral, so he has hopes for the organ, but that seems unlikely now because of necessary repair work on the Cathedral tower (D.P.G. – May 1992).

MUSIC IN BRECON CATHEDRAL

When Rees Thomas Heins retired in 1918 after a long reign as Organist - 1879-1918, he was succeeded by Ernest William Baker, an experienced Church musician who had been trained at New College School, Oxford and at Norwich Cathedral, and had moved around England from one Organist position to another with some regularity. However, it was John Humphrey Carden who was appointed first Organist and Choirmaster of Brecon Cathedral when the new diocese of Swansea and Brecon came into being on St. John's Day, 1923 whereupon St. John's Priory Church became the Cathedral.

In May 1948, the first Archdeaconry of Brecon Choral Festival was held in the Cathedral and such festivals continued on an annual basis until Humphrey Carden retired in May 1956. His successor, D. Gwerfyl Davies, found time to initiate a series of organ recitals after Evensong on Sundays, also he organised a special service sung by the combined choirs of the Cathedral and Christ College along with those of St. David's and St. Mary's Churches, Brecon on the Festival of St. Luke the Evangelist, October 18, 1958.

When Bryan Hesford was appointed as Organist, he restored weekday Choral Evensong and used for the first time, musical settings of the canticles which were brought into regular use at Cathedral services and led to an invitation from the BBC to broadcast Choral Evensong.

On his appointment as Organist of Brecon Cathedral, David Gedge organised a series of summer recitals which went on to become an annual event from 1967. That year a BBC TV "Songs of Praise" programme was broadcast, also the first town Christmas Carol Concert took place in St. Mary's Church and this too became an annual event.

During the twenty-six years that David Gedge has been Organist of Brecon Cathedral, a bewildering amount of musicmaking has taken place in the Cathedral with choral and orchestral concerts, music by visiting choirs, organ recitals by eminent recitalists such as Dr. Francis Jackson, Organist of York Minster and Christopher Dearnley, Organist of St. Paul's Cathedral and the occasional, service has been broadcast by the BBC. The choir also went out to sing in other Cathedrals such as St. David's, St. Asaph, Hereford, Worcester, Lincoln, Sheffield and St. Paul's Cathedrals. The famous choir of St. John's College, Cambridge came to Brecon to give a recital and the Royal School of Church Music course of one hundred and twenty-five choristers sang services on one Sunday in August 1971. In 1973 the Cathedral choir travelled to south Germany to sing, and in 1976 it visited Canada and the USA since when it has visited Denmark (twice) and Eire.

The Easter weekend of 1979 gave a foretaste of future Easters. On Good Friday evening during a concert, some members of the Gwent Chamber Orchestra gave a performance of J. S. Bach's Harpsichord Concerto in F minor with Hugh Thomas as soloist, then on Holy Saturday the Cathedral Singers and the orchestra performed 'Messiah' complete. The year ended with a performance of a Viennese Mass-Setting at Holy Eucharist on Christmas Day, so that from then onwards it became the custom to give the major festivals of Christmas, Easter and Whitsun a musical prominence. Furthermore J. S. Bach Cantatas now are sung at Sunday Evensongs during Advent always with soloists and with orchestral accompaniment.

In 1980, BBC TV broadcast yet another 'Songs of Praise' programme from Brecon Cathedral, and on the same day, a programme of cathedral music was broadcast on BBC Radio Wales, one of a series of programmes presented by four of the Welsh Cathedral choirs. The cathedral choir formed part of a choir of two thousand voices that led the singing at Celebration '80, a great service of Holy

Eucharist in the National Stadium, Cardiff to commemorate the diamond jubilee of The Church in Wales. The Cathedral Organist directed this combined choir while his wife Hazel Davies, played upon an electronic organ that had been installed specially for the occasion.

David Gedge finds it both remarkable and gratifying that such a continuing tradition is maintained by a voluntary choir drawn almost entirely from within the bounds of Brecon town despite its small population. The choir boys all attend local primary schools or secondary schools and on the way home call in for choir practices at the Cathedral on three evenings, staying later on Friday to sing Evensong with the lay clerks who themselves rehearse on Thursday evenings. Two services are sung by the full choir also on Sundays.

So the Cathedral continues to fulfill an important function as a centre for musical activity in the area, and the round of choral worship goes on at the Cathedral keeping alive the age-old tradition of Cathedral Music that is peculiar to Britain and the envy of the musical world. The Brecon choristers constantly strive after as high a standard as they possibly can in the hope that just occasionally, in the words of John Milton, they may 'bring all heaven before our eyes'.

These extracts from "MUSIC AT BRECON CATHEDRAL", by David Gedge are stated with his kind permission and updated in 1992.

LLANDAFF CATHEDRAL

It was about the year AD 560 that the Celtic saint Teilo reached Llandaff from West Wales, and, finding a small Christian community founded a generation earlier by Dyfrig, began to build a church on the banks of the river Taff. Llandaff Cathedral is dedicated to the Saints Peter, Paul, Dyfrig, Teilo and Euddogwy.

George Galloway Beale	1894-1936	Charles Kenneth Turner	1955-1957
William Henry Gabb	1937-1946	Eric Howard Fletcher	1957-1958
Albert Vernon Butcher	1946-1948	Robert Henry Joyce	1958-1973
Thomas Hallford	1949-1950	Michael John Smith	1974
Eric Arthur Coningsby	1950-1955		

GEORGE GALLOWAY BEALE was born in London in 1868 and was educated at Marlborough College. He was sometime a chorister there and at Westminster Abbey where he studied with J. F. Bridge. He was Organist and Assistant Master at St. John's School, Leatherhead and Organist of St. John's Church, Paddington before moving to Llandaff as Organist and Master of the Choristers in 1894. He had previously gained the Durham Mus. Bac. in 1891 and F.R.C.O. He stayed at Llandaff until his death on 7th September, 1936.

WILLIAM HARRY GABB was born on 5th April, 1909 at Ilford, Essex. He won a scholarship to study Organ and Composition at the Royal College of Music, he was winner of the Kenneth Bruce Stewart Organ Prize and the George Carter Scholarship for Organ and Composition. He gained A.R.C.O. in 1928, F.R.C.O. in 1930 and A.R.C.M. for Organ in 1931.

He was Organist of St. Jude's, West Norwood from 1925 and Organist and Choirmaster of Christ Church, Gipsy Hill, London in 1928. He became Sub-Organist of Exeter Cathedral in 1929 and also Organist of the Church of St. Leonard's, Exeter and Heavitree Parish Church from 1929-37. He was appointed Organist and Master of the Choristers at Llandaff Cathedral in 1937 and was a Lecturer at St. Michael's Theological College, Llandaff. He was in the Royal Armoured Corps during the War 1939-45.

He returned to Llandaff in 1946, but immediately returned to London as Sub-organist of St. Paul's Cathedral where he remained until 1974. He continued in this post after he was appointed as Organist of the Chapel Royal in 1953. He was Professor of Organ and Examiner at the Trinity College from 1947.

He has played at many Royal Services including the Coronation of Queen Elizabeth II and the wedding of Princess Margaret. He was created M.V.O. in 1961 and C.V.O. in 1974. He received the Mus.D., (Lambeth) in 1974. He is now Organist of Chobham Parish Church and an Hon. Fellow of the Trinity College of Music.

ALBERT VERNON BUTCHER was born in Norfolk on 11th April, 1909. He was educated at the Strand School, London. He then went to Brasenose College, Oxford as organ scholar and later to the Royal College of Music. He gained the M.A., D.Mus., and F.R.C.O. with the Lafontaine Prize and was Music Master at Chigwell School from 1930-41.

He served in the Army in the Buffs and Intelligence Corps from 1942 to 46. Appointed Organist of Llandaff Cathedral in 1946 he remained there until 1948. He then became Director of Music at Wrekin College 1949-53 and of Worcester College for the Blind 1953-74. He still lives in Worcester.

His compositions for organ include:- 'Introduction and Fugue' – published by O.U.P. and 'Three Postludes', 'Two Improvisations' – published by Hinrischen.

THOMAS HALLFORD was a pupil of Sir Edward Bairstow and took the Durham degrees of B.Mus., and D.Mus. He gained F.R.C.O., with the Lafontaine Prize and also gained the CHM diploma. In 1932 he was appointed Organist of Malton Parish Church in Yorkshire from where he moved to Alnwick and then to Brighton. He took up his post as Organist at Llandaff Cathedral in 1949. Nevil James, the Archivist of Llandaff Cathedral writes:

"The story of his time here is a mixture of great promise and cheerful hope linked with the saddest of tragedy. He succeeded Vernon Butcher in February 1949 and passages from the Llandaff Parish Magazine, written by Dean Glyn Simon (later to be Archbishop of Wales) who was also vicar of Llandaff tell much of the story."

In the month of Dr. Hallford's arrival he wrote;

"Dr. Butcher's place as Organist of the Cathedral and Master of the Choristers will be taken by Thomas Hallford, Mus.Doc., F.R.C.O., Organist of Brighton Parish Church. We offer him and Mrs Hallford and their little girl Rosemary a warm welcome. They will live in the White Cottage. Mr (sic) Hallford is a distinguished musician of whom much is expected by those qualified to judge."

Later in October he wrote:

"It is no exaggeration to say that the whole parish was saddened by the sudden deaths, within a short period of one another, of two people before whom, as it seemed, lay many years of happy life in this world...

Sylvia Hallford was an Italian lady, of a family devoted to the Allied cause in the last war. She came to Llandaff with her husband and Rosemary, and they made their first real home in the charming little cottage above St. Teilo's well.

She had already made many friends, and her death, just after the birth of twin daughters came with a sense of grievous personal loss to many people.

(Sylvia had died on 25th August, the twins having been born on 21st August). Close on the death of his wife, Dr. Hallford was plunged into the musical preparations for the enthronement of Dr. John Morgan as Archbishop of Wales at Llandaff on September 20th.

"The enthronement of the fourth Archbishop of Wales"

This event, necessarily a rare one in history of any Diocese, had the added interest this time as it took place in the nave of a Cathedral (still in ruins from enemy action in 1941...). The Archbishop's chair stood against the great white temporary screen at the east end of the Nave behind and above the Altar... the choir were ranged north and south to the east of the Altar. Trumpeters from the Royal Military School of Music at Kneller Hall were grouped to the north of the pulpit, and the organ was a Hammond organ hired for the occasion; the music was under the care of Dr. Hallford and the Cathedral Choir.

A friend of mine who was one of the choristers on that day recalls Tom Hallford trying the organ and calling for 'more power' which was duly supplied. He remembers him as a very good choir trainer who was great fun to work for.

Back to the Parish Magazine.

In the issue published in February 1950 the Dean wrote

"The death of Dr. Hallford is a great blow to music in South Wales as well as being a heavy personal loss to many friends.

He was a fine personality and those of us who had the privilege of his friendship will not easily forget his vigorous and stimulating character, his generous heart, his robust Yorkshire wit, his genius with things mechanical, his fund of tales, his impatience with the shallow or pompous.

A memorial stone was to be placed over the Hallford grave. This grave, in the cemetery near the Cathedral, bears the following inscription.

In Loving Memory of Sylvia, beloved wife of Thomas Hallford,
Born at Porto Santo Stefano, Italy 16th February, 1922.
Died at Llandaff, 25th August, 1949.
Also of Thomas Hallford – Organist of this Cathedral Church,
Born at Wath, Rotherham, 2nd July, 1911.
Died at Llandaff, 15th January, 1950.
Requiescant in Pace

The twin daughters born on 21st August, 1949 were baptised in the Cathedral by Dean Glyn Simon on 28th December, 1949 and were named Sylvia and Rose.

NEVIL JAMES

ERIC ARTHUR CONINGSBY was born on 2nd January, 1909 at Whadden, near Royston, Herts. He was educated at Cambridge and County High School and Trinity College, Cambridge gaining the B.A. degree in 1930, the M.A. in 1936, L.R.A.M. in 1935, Mus.B. in 1937 and the F.R.C.O. diploma in 1945 and CHM diploma in 1947.

He was Music Master at Bridlington School and Choirmaster of Bridlington Priory Church, 1931-32; Music Master, Glasgow Academy, 1932-36; Organist and Choirmaster, St. Matthew's Church, Glasgow, 1933-36; Organist and Choirmaster, St. Barnabas Church, Cambridge and Conductor of the Cambridge Philharmonic Society, 1937-40.

He was a Meteorologist with the RAF, 1940-44. On leaving the RAF he became temporary Assistant Music Master at Uppingham School from 1945, before becoming Organist and Choirmaster at Folkestone Parish Church, Kent, 1945-50 and Conductor of the Folkestone Orpheus Choir and Orchestra as well as being Conductor of the Dover Choral Society.

In 1950 he came to Llandaff as Organist and Master of the Choristers. He left Llandaff in 1952, becoming Organist of Grimsby Parish Church in 1954 and he died on 22nd September, 1955.

CHARLES KENNETH TURNER was born in 1904 in Crosby, Liverpool. Malcolm Cousins, Organist of Mansfield Parish Church, Nottinghamshire has kindly supplied the following notes taken from a newspaper cutting reporting the death of C. Kenneth Turner on 2nd January, 1959.

"C. Kenneth Turner was appointed Organist of Mansfield Parish Church only 14 months ago. A native of Crosby, Liverpool, he was educated at the Merchant Tailors' School and the Guildhall School of Music. His first organist's post was at Brasted, Kent at 15 years.

"Before going to Llandaff Cathedral, he was Organist of Maidstone Parish Church, Kent for 7 years. He was a teacher at University College of Cardiff and of St. Michael's Theological College, Llandaff. Since coming to Mansfield he had been able to devote time to composing, organ, piano music; songs and choral pieces."

Mr Cousins adds that a few of his MSS are in the St. Peter's Choir library in Mansfield.

Turner held several organists' posts before moving to Llandaff Cathedral in 1952 as Organist and Master of the Choristers. These were, Walton-on-Thames Parish Church, 1924-9, St. John's, Redhill, Surrey, 1929-34, St. Peter's, Croydon, 1934-7, and again at St. John's, Redhill, Surrey from 1937. Whilst at Llandaff he was also Organist of Llandaff Parish Church.

He was described as being 'one of nature's gentlemen, a most loyal colleague and utterly devoted to his work'.

ERIC HOWARD FLETCHER was born in Essex on 19th December, 1933. He is M.A., Mus.B. (Cantab), F.R.C.O. Previous to his appointment as Organist and Master of the Music at Llandaff Cathedral, he was educated at Haileybury and Pembroke College, Cambridge, where he was Organ Scholar, 1954-57. He studied with Dr. Hubert Middleton, Professor Patrick Hadley, Thurston Dart and Dr. Boris Ord.

In his final year he assisted in the conduct of daily rehearsals and services under Boris Ord's direction, in the Chapel of King's College, Cambridge as well as serving as accompanist to CUMS Chorus and the University Madrigal Society for their 1957 Leiden Tour. He took part in broadcasts and a recording with the Choir of King's College, featuring especially the music of Herbert Howells including the first broadcast of the Collegium Regale communion service, and the Argo recording – an Easter Matins – of the Collegium Regale Te Deum and Jubilate.

He took consultation organ lessons with George Guest, Sir John Dykes Bower and Lady Susi Jeans. He was Organist and Master of the Choristers at Llandaff Cathedral from 1957-58.

Whilst at Llandaff, he collaborated with Sir William McKie (Westminster Abbey) in the detailed tonal design of the new Cathedral organ, and was influential on the committee which set up the first Llandaff Cathedral Festival of Music, the new organ was inaugurated by Jeanne Demessieux, and was featured in a Handel concerto, with The Philomusica of London, conducted by Thurston Dart. Mr Fletcher was also Conductor of the Cathedral Special Choir, and a teacher at Cardiff College of Music and Drama, and at the University College, Cardifff.

Following his Llandaff period, he was Sub-organist of Peterborough Cathedral and Assistant Conductor of Peterborough Philharmonic Society, 1959-60.

Subsequently he was Assistant at Westminster Cathedral combining these responsibilities with daily teaching at the Guildhall School of Music and work in adult education, as a Music Tutor for the Extra-Mural Department of the University of London. He was also Organist at Kingsway Hall, working under Dr. Donald (now Lord) Soper.

From 1972 to 1988 he was resident in USA, initially as a teacher at Susquehanna University, where he headed the Organ and Choral Departments, and at Dickinson College, Carlisle, Pa.

From 1974 he was based in New York City, and was active as an organist, conductor and teacher there; he founded the Church Music Center and was in demand as an academic advisor to American educational institutions on music literature – music in print and recorded music.

He set up a major distribution organisation, supplying Universities, Libraries and Churches, coast to coast from his unique collection of music repertoire, recordings and books on music; establishing also his own publishing company, championing the best of British and American composers, and restoring many organ and choral (Cathedral repertoire) works to current availability.

He continues this work, now back in the UK as one of the country's few remaining specialist suppliers. His compositions include Church and Organ music. His publications are articles on Renaissance and Baroque Music, and on the Organ in Llandaff Cathedral.

ROBERT HENRY JOYCE was born in Tynemouth, Northumberland on 20th October, 1927 and was educated at Tynemouth High School. From 1944 to 1946 he studied at the Royal College of Music with an Organ Scholarship. He was a pupil of William Harris, Harold Darke and C. Thornton Lofthouse. From 1946 to 49 he was Organ Scholar at Corpus Christi College, Cambridge where he gained M.A., and Mus.B., and where he studied as an organ pupil of Boris Ord the organist of Kings College.

He was back at the Royal College of Music 1949-50 as a member of the Conducting class under Richard Austin. In 1950-58 he was Organist of St. Matthew's, Northampton and Conductor of the Northampton Bach Choir and the Northampton Symphony Orchestra.

He came to Llandaff Cathedral as Organist and Master of the Choristers in 1958 and was Conductor of the Cathedral Choral Society. Since 1974 he has been Senior Lecturer at the Welsh College of Music and Drama, Cardiff having left the Cathedral in 1973.

He is a tutor both for the Open University and for the Extra-Mural Department of the University College of Wales, Cardiff. He has been an Examiner for the Associated Board of the Royal Schools of Music since 1966, a Member of the Royal College of Organists Council 1967-79, a Member of the A.R.C.O. Board, 1972-74 and a Member of the F.R.C.O. Board 1978-80. His other qualifications are:- A.D.C.M., F.R.C.O. (CHM), A.R.C.M. His special studies are:- Church Music, Organ and Orchestral conducting.

MICHAEL JOHN SMITH was born in Wanstead, Essex on 7th June, 1937. He gained his performers' L.R.A.M. as a pianist at the age of 15 and two organ diplomas before leaving school for the University of Oxford, where he succeeded Christopher Robinson as Organ Scholar of Christ Church. He won the Limpus Prize with the F.R.C.O. Diploma.

He founded the Christ Church – St. Hilda's Music Society, and stayed for a fourth year, acquiring the postgraduate degree of B.Mus. in Composition. After a further year at London University Institute of Education, he succeeded Andrew Seivewright as Organist of Pontefract Parish Church and Head of Music at the King's School. Four years later he succeeded Michael Nicholas at St. James' Church and King Edward VI Grammar School, Louth, Lincolnshire.

During this period he gained. the A.D.C.M. and was a finalist in two successive years at the St. Albans International Organ Festival. In 1967 he was appointed Assitant Choirmaster and Organist at Salisbury Cathedral, working with both Christopher Dearnley and Richard Seal.

While there, he married Marian Cooper (a graduate of the Royal Academy of Music), studied for the Edinburgh degree of D. Mus as an executant, and conducted a number of concerts given by Salisbury Musical Society. He was much involved at this time with teaching both privately and in local shools, and with the work of the R.S.C.M., and also became an Associated Board examiner. He also became well-known as a recitalist, playing in half the cathedrals of England and Wales.

In 1974 Dr. Smith was appointed Organist and Master of the Choristers at Llandaff Cathedral and Conductor of the Cathedral Choral Society. During the next 17 years he conducted fifty concerts with the Society, mostly with the BBC Welsh Symphony Orchestra, exploring the choral repertory from the 17th Century to the present day, and in 1986 was co-conductor of the first Cardiff performance of Britten's 'War Requiem', in St. David's Hall. Dr. Smith played at the opening concert of the Hall in 1983, and at its inaugural organ recital. In the Cathedral he has promoted several three-choir concerts, combining forces with Bath Abbey, Bristol Cathedral and Wells Cathedral.

In 1983 he was elected to the Council of the Royal College of Organists and he has been a tutor at University College, Cardiff, the Welsh College of Music and Drama, St. Michael's Theological College and the Cathedral School. Since 1987 he has directed the Cardiff Tallis Singers. Examining tours have taken him twice to Malaysia and to Singapore, Hong Kong, South Africa, Mauritius and New Zealand.

He has a son and two daughters, with whom he enjoys pottering about in his 17th Century cottage in Herefordshire, cycling and camping, when time allows.

LLANDAFF CATHEDRAL: The Organ

LLANDAFF CATHEDRAL ORGAN – early history

The following extract is taken from 'Cathedral Organists, Past and Present', by John E. West:- Very scanty records exist of the earlier Organists of Llandaff Cathedral. For some considerable period both the fabric and the establishment had been in a declining state, and in 1691 the Choir was suppressed and the organ destroyed. As a substitute, the National Schoolmaster was appointed to lead the singing, for which he received £4 per annum. At Bishop Ollivant's enthronement, on March 13th, 1850, these crippled musical arrangements appear to have been still in force, for we read that "On the opening of the door to the bishop's summons... the National Schoolmaster, heading the procession, gave out a Psalm, which was sung by about a dozen of his scholars, a bass viol being the only instrument then in the possession of the Cathedral. In this way the bishop was conducted to his throne." (Bishop's Charge, 1869).

Under the rule of this worthy prelate Choral Service was re-established in 1861, having been discontinued from 1691 until 1861.

The recent history of the organs of Llandaff Cathedral dates back to 1861, when an instrument was installed by Gray and Davison at the time of the restoration of the building, which for a century and a half had been in ruins. At the turn of the century that organ was sold to Usk Parish Church, where it remains to this day, and a new organ was designed in 1898 by Hope Jones.

At the time of the actual building, it seems that the firm had been taken over by Norman and Beard, though the name-plate on the console recorded only the name of Hope Jones.

It was the first organ in South Wales to embody the use of electro-pneumatic action, but whereas its predecessor had a specification including a full diapason chorus on both Great and Swell divisions (with mixtures of four and three ranks respectively), the new instrument, also of three manuals, possessed no stop above 4′ pitch, and was typical of the degenerative nature of the British organ at this period.

Some years later, probably in 1914, Messrs Norman and Beard added the Solo organ and made a few alterations, bringing the number of speaking stops to thirty-four, but still without mixtures and mutations.

This instrument was extensively rebuilt in 1938 by Messrs Hill, Norman and Beard, with the addition of some upperwork on the Great and Swell but no improvement in the Pedal division.

In January 1941 a landmine fell in the churchyard, causing serious damage to the Cathedral and putting the building out of action, except for the Lady Chapel and Sanctuary, for the next sixteen years. For five years there was nothing but a one-manual Mustel organ, blown by operating a pedal, until in 1946 a two-manual organ by Hill (from the Roman Catholic church at Eastcote) was moved into the Lady Chapel.

When the Nave was restored in 1957, this small instrument was moved to a bay of the south arcade, and meanwhile, plans were made to salvage what was left of the main organ and to add certain new stops in order to bring it into line with current thinking about the so-called 'classical organ'.

The work was again assigned to Hill, Norman and Beard, whose chief concession to modern practice was the installation of a Positive division, situated with striking visual effect in a concrete cylindrical case atop a parabolic arch, also in concrete, which was set up by architect George Pace between the Nave and the Choir.

Pace had conceived this department as a means of leading congregational singing, but its specification is quite unsuitable for this purpose, just as its position is unsuitable for its proper use as a Positive organ, which should be in the main case. The rest of the organ largely survived, with various additions which left it as the hotch-potch it is today.

In 1977 Dr. Michael Smith made representations to the Chapter that the time had come for a new organ, or at least a thorough rebuild, removing the worst stops and making the most of the remainder. Cecil Clutton was appointed to advise the Chapter, and four notable organ-builders came to inspect the organ, two of them providing interesting and far-reaching new specifications.

Alas, the Chapter adopted a negative approach and settled instead for the introduction of solid-state action and a repair of the wind-supply, thereby perpetuating a basically poor instrument for a few more decades.

Llandaff Cathedral have also a Bates chamber organ c.1800.

MJS

LLANDAFF CATHEDRAL: The Choral Foundation

The origins of music at Llandaff are lost in the mists of time, dating back perhaps for a thousand years, but the tradition has not been maintained continuously through the centuries, owing to the chequered history of the cathedral's fortunes.

The Choir School was refounded by Dean Vaughan in 1880, and since then the choristers have all been educated there as boarders. The school now occupies the Georgian building which was once the Bishop's Palace, and has over 400 pupils, of whom about a quarter are girls.

The Cathedral Choir consists of 14 choristers, 6 lay clerks and 3 choral scholars. Evensong is sung every day except Wednesday during term-time, the Monday and Friday services being sung by boys only. Until quite recently, the Sunday morning service alternated between Matins and the Eucharist, but Matins has been gradually phased out to leave a Eucharist every Sunday, thereby increasing the demand for a wide repertoire of settings.

These include Latin masses by Haydn, Mozart and Schubert, together with English settings by composers such as Stanford, Darke, Vaughan Williams, Jackson, Leighton, Mathias, Simon Preston and Robert Walker; about 25 settings in all.

During the course of a year, about 90 settings of the evening canticles are sung (most appearing only twice) and there is a repertoire of about 300 anthems in regular use, in addition to fifteen settings of the Responses. The maintenance of so much music entails about nine hours' rehearsal per week, and there are about 260 sung services in a year.

The Assistant Organist, Michael Hoeg, was appointed in 1980 and is Director of Music at the Cathedral School. The lay clerks come from various walks of life, while the Choral Scholars are students either at the University College in Cardiff or the Welsh College of Music and Drama. During the '80s the choir made four records on the Alpha label and gave concerts in France, Holland and Sweden.

MJS

ST. WOOLOS CATHEDRAL

About AD500, Gwynllwg's church was built. Woolos is an English corruption of Gwynllwg! The present building which became the Cathedral Church of St. Woolos, Newport, is built on top of a ridge which dominates the town.

The Diocese was created in 1921 from the Diocese of Llandaff, the church being given Pro-Cathedral status, and in 1949, full Cathedral status was achieved. (Taken from St. Woolos Cathedral Guide Book, notes by the Revd. Andrew Willie, M.A.)

ST. WOOLOS CATHEDRAL ORGANISTS

John Augustus Gaccon	1894-1934	Donald William Bate	1964-1978
Cyril James Ball	1934-1941	Christopher Michael John Barton	1979
Charles St. Ervan Johns	1941-1963		

NEWPORT – THE CATHEDRAL CHURCH OF ST. WOOLOS – DIOCESE OF MONMOUTH

The information about the musical life of the Cathedral Church is taken from *Music at St. Woolos'*: Some historical notes by Donald Bate, with his kind permission.

"When in 1921 the Diocese of Monmouth was created, the ancient Parish Church of Newport became the Pro-Cathedral. In 1949 it was named as the Cathedral Church of the Diocese, and to meet its new role effectively the east end of the church was extended in the 1960s.

No one can say with certainty what music was provided for the church in earlier days, although it is probable that in the eighteenth century the hymns were sung to the accompaniment of a violin, bass viol and flute; or the parish clerk would sing a line and the congregation repeat it.

However, in 1819 an organ was built and erected by Mr Smith of Bristol. He was the founder of Messrs Vowles and Son, a firm well known throughout Wales and the west of England. The organ was small and was placed on a gallery then called the 'Singing Gallery', which stood in the east end of the nave over the entrance to the chancel. There was ample room in the gallery for a large choir. The Organist in 1819 was a Mr Davis.

In 1824 the Reverend W. W. Isaacson, an outstanding figure in the history of St. Woolos Church, with an evident desire to improve the standard of the music, introduced a service book, the title-page of which reads: "A Selection of Psalms, from the Authorised version, with a few Hymns and Anthems, expressly arranged for the service of the Parish Church of Newport, alias Saint Woolos – by a clergyman". This service book met with favour, for a second edition was produced in 1830.

In November, 1833, Mr Wall of Chepstow was appointed organist in the room of Mr Hall. A tombstone in St. Woolos' churchyard stated that T. R. Price was for nineteen years the much respected and efficient organist of this church. He was appointed in 1834.

About 1840, considerable additions and improvements were made to the organ. In 1855, the church was reopened after extensive repairs and improvements. The singing gallery was taken down and a new chancel arch erected. It was the intention of the responsible committee to place the organ in the eastern end of the north aisle, but a strong memorial signed by the majority of the pew holders induced the committee to consent it to the erection of a special gallery at the west end of the church to receive it.

The organ was repaired and enlarged. It was erected by a Mr Godard, but the large pedal pipes were made by Mr Gregory, the verger of the church. Some of these pedal pipes are still in use in the present instrument.

The opening service took place in 1858. The organist was Mr H. J. Groves, who had been appointed in 1853 in place of Mr Price. The music selected for the opening services included settings of the Te Deum laudamus and Jubilate Deo by Mendelssohn and of the Cantate Domino and Deus misereatur by William Hayes; and the anthems 'The Lord is very great' and 'O where shall wisdom be found?' by, respectively, Beckwith and Boyce. It is recorded that the choir, augmented for the occasion, sang with profound effect.

In 1878, the organ was again moved, and re-erected, with additions and improvements in the Crindau Chapel (north aisle) by Mr Vowles of Bristol at a cost of about £500. Later a surpliced choir was introduced and led the singing from a raised platform immediately in front of the organ. The gallery at the west end of the nave was subsequently removed. Meanwhile, the book now known as 'Hymns Ancient and Modern' was adopted, together with 'The Cathedral Psalter'.

Mr S. Round was appointed Organist about 1885. He was followed by Mr Edward Dean who resigned in 1893. Mr J. A. Gaccon was appointed in 1894 (see his biographical details).

Certain alterations and additions were made to the organ in 1895. In 1915 the organ was rebuilt by Messrs Griffen and Stroud of Bath, most of the pipes from the previous instrument being incorporated into the new one. The organ again was moved – this time to the chancel.

This organ, of three manuals and pedals had thirty-four stops (twenty-six speaking, seven containing couplers and a tremulant), the great organ containing seven stops, the swell organ ten stops, the choir organ five stops and the pedal organ four.

Mr Gaccon was succeeded in 1934 by Mr C. J. Ball; and Mr C. St. Ervan Johns was organist from 1941 to 1963.

In 1960, to enable work to proceed on the Cathedral extensions, the Griffen and Stroud organ was removed and for two years, a grand piano was used to accompany the services.

Her Majesty Queen Elizabeth II visited the church on 26th October, 1962. Earlier in the month, in readiness for the visit, Messrs Hill, Norman and Beard installed the five-stop chapel organ, playable from a temporary one-manual stop-key console with pedals operated only through the manual keys. The chapel organ, which is south of the chancel, is now playable from the main console.

The present organ was dedicated by the Archbishop of Wales on St. Luke's Day, Tuesday 18th October, 1966, the forty-fifth anniversary of the creation of the diocese of Monmouth. Built by Messrs Hill, Norman and Beard, the instrument incorporates most of the Hill organ formerly in Newport Town Hall, with the exception of the pedal department. Much of the pedal section is from the former cathedral organ, as this section was more adaptable to the limited space available. It is known as St. Johns organ after C. St. Ervan Johns.

Mr Bate then goes on to give more details about the wind pressure and also a complete specification of the organ together with a photograph of the console at St. Woolos. He gives the credit of much of the material in his article having been extracted from notes compiled by the late Mr J. A. Gaccon, and finally expresses his thanks to the Dean of Monmouth for permission to make use of the material presented, and I, in turn, express my thanks to these gentlemen and to Mr Bate.

REPRINTED FROM WELSH MUSIC, VOL III, NO. 5, AUTUMN 1969

JOHN AUGUSTUS GACCON was born in Cardiff on 5th November, 1869 and received his musical education locally. He was Organist of St. John the Baptist's Church, Newport before his appointment to St. Woolos Church, Newport in 1894.

He was successful in the Royal College of Organists diplomas in 1908 when he gained the Fellowship Diploma. He became Newport Borough Organist and was Music Master of Newport High Schools from 1895 until his death on 28th April, 1934, as well as holding the Cathedral post. He was Grand Organist of the Grand Lodge of England and Grand Organist of the Grand Chapter Royal Arch Freemasons. J. A. Gaccon was also A.R.C.M.

Mr John Gaccon, Junior, played for a few months in the interim.

CYRIL JAMES BALL was born at Wellington, Shropshire on 6th April, 1905 and he was educated at Queen Mary's Grammar School, Walsall and Lady Lumley's Grammar School, Pickering and Archbishop Holgate's School, York. He served his articles to Edward C. Bairstow at York Minister, 1924-28.

He gained the F.R.C.O., diploma in 1927 with the Lafontaine Prize and Silver Medal of the Worshipful Company of Musicians and was successful in the Durham degree of B.Mus., in 1928 gaining the CHM diploma in 1929. He spent some time in private practice as a teacher of music before taking up the appointment as Organist and Master of the Choristers at St. Woolos Cathedral in 1934 also being Music Master of Newport Grammar School and Borough Organist of Newport like his predecessor, J. A. Gaccon.

He left Newport in 1941 and entered Edinburgh University and took the degrees of B.D. and D.Mus. in 1947. He was then ordained in the Church of Scotland and served for a year (1947-8) as assistant minister at Dunfermline Abbey.

From 1948 to 1952 he was County Music Organiser for Caithness, and from 1952 to 1959 he served as minister of Hutton and Corrie, Dumfriesshire. In 1957 he took the Edinburgh degree of Ph.D., and from 1959 to 1967 was Head of the Music Department at Winneba Training College, Ghana. He then returned to Scotland where he died on 6th November, 1975.

CHARLES ST. ERVAN JOHNS was born in Manchester on 22nd October, 1896 and was educated at Swansea Grammar School being also a chorister at St. James' Church there. He held early organ appointments at St. Barnabas' and St. James' Churches in Swansea and at St. Mary's Church, Chepstow.

In 1921 he was appointed to St. John's, Maindee, Newport, where he remained until his appointment to St. Woolos Cathedral in 1941. In that same year he also became Borough Organist of Newport like his two predecessors, and in 1945 he was appointed Music Adviser to the Borough. Johns held the F.R.C.O. diploma (1917), A.R.C.M. He died at Newport, Monmouthshire, on 6th July, 1963.

DONALD WILLIAM BATE was born in Cardiff on 14th September, 1912 and attended Cardiff High School. He had been an Organist since 1928 at several Cardiff churches and was Organist and Choirmaster of St. Woolos Cathedral, Newport, Gwent from 1st January, 1964 to 30th November, 1978.

Before this appointment, he says, it was his privilege for many years to play for occasional services at Llandaff Cathedral and to take occasional choir practices. In 1938 he won the organ playing prize at the Welsh National Eisteddfod held in Cardiff. He is an experienced organ recitalist and used to give frequent public recitals.

As a part-time tutor on the staff of the music department of the Welsh College of Music and Drama from 1949 to 1985, he was responsible for a great part of the organ tuition at the College. He taught music privately (part-time) from about 1935 until war service intervened.

He has considerable experience in choral training with both young people and adults. He was conductor for the Monmouthshire Diocesan Choral Association and conducted or played for many other church music festivals. He has adjudicated at many eisteddfodau and has had a wide experience as a lecturer to music clubs and similar organisations.

During the war he did a great deal of work for ENSA, particularly as a pianist, with good music parties in the Middle East. A captain with Security Intelligence in Egypt, he became Officer-in-Charge, Security Identification Section, 18 (Canal) Area, Middle East Forces. An experienced piano accompanist, he has served in this capacity, and as an organist for the BBC and T.W.W.

He was for many years secretary of the Cardiff and District Organ Club and frequently arranged large-scale public organ recitals. He gained the F.R.C.O. diploma in 1958. He also holds the L.R.A.M. diploma (piano), L.T.C.L (organ).

Employed by the South Wales Electricity Board (Senior Commercial Assistant), he took early retirement.

In the 1930s he won several public speaking competitions, was secretary of a dramatic society and took part on stage. Since his marriage in 1936 he has been a keen gardener. All his life his chief relaxation has been in walking, long hours roaming the country-side especially in the hills.

CHRISTOPHER MICHAEL JOHN BARTON was born in London, 8th February, 1956 and was educated at the Royal Grammar School, High Wycombe (1966-1971) and Trent College, Nottingham (1971-1972), before going to Worcester College, Oxford as organ scholar (1975-1978).

On coming down from Oxford he started a teacher training course at the University of London Institute of Education, but was unable to complete this due to his appointment as Organist and Master of the Choristers at St. Woolos Cathedral with effect from January 1979. He studied organ with James Dalton and Richard Popplewell, and composition with Edmund Rubbra. His professional qualifications are M.A., F.R.C.O. (CHM), A.D.C.M., L.R.A.M.

With the cathedral choir he has been responsible for the music at many important provincial services, including the Consecrations of two bishops and the Enthronements of an archbishop and a bishop.

The choir has also performed extensively in England, in venues from Exeter to York, and it has toured Holland, Germany and Canada. It also has three recordings and a number of broadcasts to its credit, including appearances on British and Canadian television. Despite all this activity, though, it never forgets that its primary duty is leading the regular worship offered at the cathedral.

His compositions include:- Evening Service; St. Cadoc Service; anthem 'Holy is the True Light', and a Communion setting.

Since 1985, Christopher Barton has also been Music Director of the Dyfed Choir, one of the leading mixed voice choirs in the United Kingdom, another choir with many broadcasts to its credit. With this choir he has performed a very wide repertoire, including several baroque works with orchestras of period instruments.

In addition to this work as a practical performer, he has a strong commitment to teaching and an increasing interest in composition. His hobbies include almost all genres of 'serious' music, including jazz, the arts in general and English literature in particular, languages (learning Welsh), playing racquet sports, watching other sports especially cricket, following politics and current affairs (in the abstract, not as a party politician) and enjoying the countryside.

ST. WOOLOS CATHEDRAL CHOIR

St. Woolos Cathedral maintains a voluntary, i.e. unpaid choir of boys and men. The choristers attend a number of junior and secondary schools in and around Newport, while the gentlemen of the choir follow a number of professions, teaching being particularly well represented. At any given time in the choir there is also a number of former choristers, teenage boys now singing alto, tenor or bass.

The prime responsibility of the choir is the maintenance of the regular sung worship of the cathedral; two services are sung on Sundays, and Choral Evensong is sung on Wednesdays by the choristers and on Fridays by the full choir.

Special services are sung in Advent and at Christmas, in Holy Week and on other particularly significant days in the Church Year. In addition the choir has musical responsibility for such important diocesan occasions as Ordinations, Installations of Canons, etc.

The choir frequently performs outside its own cathedral, either singing services or giving concerts. It tours regularly and has sung in cathedrals from Exeter to York (three times), as well as in Holland, Germany and Canada.

It has also appeared several times in television, including Canadian television, and been heard on radio, including in a concert performance of William Mathias' *This worldes joie*, conducted by the composer.

An extremely wide repertouire is sung, ranging from plainsong (plainsong canticles normally being used on Wednesdays) to specially commissioned music from composers such as William Mathias, Herbert Sumsion, Philip Moore, Richard Shephard. Robert Ashfield, Adrian Williams several others. At the time of writing three recordings have been made, and more are planned.

Away from the stalls the choir has an active social life, with regular non-singing holidays and day trips for the choristers, from Truro to York, from St. David's to Cambridge; these are seen as being very important in helping to cement the happy relationships necessary in any choir, but especially in one which demands so much time from its choristers on a completely voluntary basis.

ST. ASAPH CATHEDRAL
EGLWYS GADEIRIOL LLANELWY

In an age only dimly outlined, we learn of the first religious establishment on the south bank of the river Elwy by Cyndeyrn (Kentigern), the exiled bishop from Strathclyde in Scotland in A.D. 560. Asaph succeeded Cyndryrn as bishop after the latter's return to Scotland and it was Asaph who gave his name to the Cathedral and Diocese.

Taken from St. Asaph Cathedral Guide Book.

ST. ASAPH CATHEDRAL ORGANISTS

Archibald Wayett Wilson	1898-1901	James Roland Middleton	1963-1970
Cyril Bradley Rootham	1901-1901	Graham John Elliott	1970-1981
William Edward Belcher	1901-1917	John Theodore Belcher	1981-1985
Harold Carpenter Lumb Stocks	1917-1956	Hugh H. Davies	1985
Robert Duke Dickinson	1956-1962		

ARCHIBALD WAYETT WILSON was born on 8th August, 1869 at Pinchbeck, Lincolnshire. He was educated at Rossall School, Lancashire. He was a student at the Royal College of Music under Sir Walter Parratt and Sir Frederick Bridge.

He was Organist of East Moulsey in 1888, and then he became Organ student at Keble College, Oxford 1890. He became Mus.D., (Oxon) and F.R.C.O. He was Music Master of Temple Grove Eastbourne from 1898, Organist of St. John's Church, St. Leonard's Sussex in 1896 and Organist of St. Asaph Cathedral in 1898 and Ely Cathedral in 1901.He was appointed Organist of Manchester Cathedral in 1919 remaining until 1943.

His degrees were gained:- Mus.B. 1891, B.A. 1893, Mus.D. 1897, M.A. 1913.

He was a composer of a Choral Ballad, part-songs and Church Music. He became Organist Emeritus of Manchester Cathedral and he died on 17th August, 1950

CYRIL BRADLEY ROOTHAM, was born on 5th October, in 1875 in Bristol and was educated at Bristol Grammar School, Clifton College and St. John's College, Cambridge, (Classical and Musical Scholarships), and at the Royal College of Music. He gained the B.A. (Classical Tripos), 1897, Mus. Bac. 1900, M.A. 1901, Mus. Doc. 1910.

He was Organist of Christ Church, Hampstead, from 1898, and of St. Asaph Cathedral from February to October 1901, whereupon he became a Fellow and Organist of St. John's College, Cambridge. He lectured before the International Congress of Musicians in London in 1911.

He was a Fellow of the Royal College of Music and Examiner for musical degrees at Cambridge University. He became University Lecturer in Form and Analysis of Music, 1913-1918 and University Lecturer in Harmony and Counterpoint, 1924-38.

He was College Lecturer in Music in 1919 and Conductor of the University Musical Society, 1912-36.

He conducted performances in the Cambridge Theatre of Mozart's 'Magic Flute', 1911, Purcell's 'Fairy Queen', 1920 and 1931, Cyril Rootham's 'The Two Sisters' 1922, Handel's 'Semele', 1925, Purcell's 'King Arthur', 1928. He lectured twice at the Royal Institute, 1926.

He exercised a strong influence upon the cultivation of Music at the University. He was Organist of St. John's College at the time of his death on 18th March, 1938.

His publications were numerous, including 'Andromeda', a dramatic cantata, Laurence Binyon's 'For The Fallen', for chorus and orchestra; instrumental music and setting's of choruses from Robert Bridge's 'Archilles in Scyros'; numerous songs and part-songs; Four Dramatic Songs (with words by Mary Coleridge) for high voice and orchestra; The Two Sisters, opera; Suite for Strings and Pianoforte; Dances for strings from Purcell's 'Fairy Queen'; Thomas Moult's 'Brown Earth', for chorus, semi-chorus and orchestra; String Quartet in C Major; Rhapsody on an old English Tune for double string orchestra; Violin and Pianoforte Sonata in G Minor; Milton's 'Ode on the Morning of Christ's Nativity', for soloists, chorus and semi-chorus and orchestra; Trio for violin, violoncello and pianoforte; several orchestral works, including a Symphony in C Minor, and a Septet for viola, harp and wind instruments still in manuscript. Psalm CIII for chorus and orchestra.

He published a book 'Voice Training for Chorus and Schools', and various musical pamphlets.

WILLIAM EDWARD BELCHER was born at Handsworth, Birmingham in 1864. He was the son of a Birmingham musician, Thomas Belcher, D.Mus. (Oxon). Belcher was educated at King Edward's School, Birmingham and then became a student at the Royal College of Music and a Choral Scholar at King's College, Cambridge where he gained the B.A. in 1887 and the M.A. in 1891.

He became an F.R.C.O. in 1892 and then A.R.C.M. He became Organist of the Parish Church of Kingston-on-Thames in 1891. He taught Music and Mathematics at Bromsgrove School 1889-91 and became Organist of St. Michael's, Headingley, Leeds in 1893 and Deputy-Organist to the Leeds Corporation, 1895. In 1901 he came to St. Asaph as Cathedral Organist in October, resigning the post in 1917. He was a composer of church music.

HAROLD CARPENTER LUMB STOCKS was born on 21st October, 1884 at Essendon, Hertfordshire and was educated at St. Asaph Grammar School. He studied music under Dr. A. W. Wilson and others, and gained the Mus.B. (Oxon) 1911, Mus.D. (Dublin) 1921, and F.R.C.O. He was Organist of Littleport Parish Church near Ely in 1902.

Then followed a time as Organist of St. Mary's, Ely and as Assistant Organist of Ely Cathedral from 1906. He moved to Yeovil Parish Church in 1909 and was conductor of Yeovil Choral Society, moving to Ludlow Parish Church in 1911.

He was invalided from the Army in 1916 after service with the R.A.M.C. in Salonika and Egypt. He was appointed Organist of St. Asaph in 1917, and remained until his death on 10th February, 1956.

When the Cathedral Organists Association was founded by Dr. Charles Macpherson and Dr. Sydney H. Nicholson in 1919 he was firstly Hon. Treasurer from 1921 and then Hon. Secretary from 1933.

Dr. Stocks compiled a book, 'British Cathedral and Collegiate Organists', which, apart from a complete list of Cathedral Organists up to 1949, includes information about the Cathedral Organists' Association, British Diplomas and other Musical Distinctions, Organ Builders and Part Makers, the Incorporated Association of Organists, the Royal College of Organists, the Royal School of Church Music, Masters of the King's Music, Musical Knightage, British University Professors of Music and Degrees and Hoods, which must have been a very useful source of information when it was published.

His list of publications was extensive:- 'Missa Sancti Asaph', Communion Service in E flat; Evening Services in E minor, D major and D minor; Welsh Communion Service in E minor; Anthems:- As Now the Sun's Declining Rays; Thus Saith the Lord; Let Saints on Earth; Breathe on Me, Breath of God; Lord of All Being; O Gladsome Light; Grant we Beseech Thee; a Service Book for Use in Choral Festivals; songs; part-songs; O Breathe not his name; I Arise from Dreams of Thee; Barbara Allen (arranged for Soprano, Alto, Tenor and Bass); Chamber Music; A Wessex Pastorale for Clarinet and Piano; Seventeen Duets with Five Finger Basses; Variations for Organ on Y Delyn Aur; an edited Bach's Pastorale, Jig and edited Corelli Fugues.

Other books written by Dr. Stocks were:- 'The Training of Boy Choristers' and 'A Beginner's Book on Counterpoint'.

Following the death of Dr. Stocks, Mr Douglas Smith, his pupil, acted as Organist until the arrival of the new Organist, Robert Dickinson. Douglas Smith now lives in retirement in Cheltenham where he helped found the Cheltenham Symphony Orchestra with which he regularly plays Mozart Piano Concertos.

ROBERT DUKE DICKINSON was born in Liverpool on 16th November, 1916. He was educated privately and took the B.Mus. degree of Durham in 1945, and he holds the F.R.C.O. and CHM Diplomas and the L.R.A.M.

Several Organists posts were held by Robert Dickinson: St. Stephen the Martyr, Liverpool, 1933-36, Huyton Parish Church, Lancs., 1938-41, and St. Agnes' Church, Sefton Park, Liverpool, 1941-44.

In 1944 he was appointed part-time Music Master at Mold Grammar School and Organist of Mold Parish Church. Also he conducted the Senior School Orchestra, Howell's Girls' School, Denbigh from 1947. He was a lecturer for the W.E.A. as well as for the Extra-Mural Departments of Birmingham, Bangor, Surrey, Liverpool and London Universities following his move from Lancashire to the Midlands and then back to North Wales and so to Surrey.

In 1950 he became Organist of Leamington Spa Parish Church, remaining in Leamington until his appointment to St. Asaph Cathedral in 1956. He left St. Asaph in 1962 and became Director of Music at St. Catherine's School, Bramley, Guildford until his retirement in 1982.

Over a period of years Dickinson broadcast organ recitals for the BBC regional programmes and for the Third Programme whilst at Leamington Spa and St. Asaph.

Now in semi-retirement, he plays the organ at St. Michael and St. George Garrison Church, Aldershot and is involved in occasional free-lance playing at other churches in the Farnham area. He has additionally a 'comfortable' amount of private teaching in Organ and Piano.

The Acting Organist of St. Asaph Cathedral on the departure of Mr Dickinson was Miss Maureen Robinson.

JAMES ROLAND MIDDLETON was born on 8th March, 1895 at Ringwood, Hampshire and was educated privately. He was Organist of Kinson Parish Church 1914-15, and of Ringwood Parish Church 1915-22 and also of Mold Parish Church 1923-44, during the period, 1934-44, being also the Sub-organist of Chester Cathedral. He gained the B.Mus. degree in 1929 and the D.Mus. degree in 1935 and he also held the F.R.C.O. and F.T.C.L. diplomas. He was appointed Organist of Chelmsford Cathedral in 1945 but soon moved back to Chester Cathedral as Organist in 1949. He stayed at Chester Cathedral until 1963, moving then to St. Asaph Cathedral as Organist until 1970. He died at St. Asaph on 13th April 1983.

He was at sometime an examiner for the Trinity College of Music and a Member of the Royal College of Organists.

GRAHAM JOHN ELLIOTT was born 10th November, 1947 at Abergavenny, Wales. He was educated at the Royal Academy of Music where he was a composition and organ student. He was subsequently organ student at St. George's Chapel, Windsor Castle. He previously studied organ with Dr. Melville Cook at Hereford Cathedral.

Following a short period as Sub-Organist of Llandaff Cathedral in 1967-70 he was appointed Organist of St. Asaph Cathedral, at which time he was the youngest Cathedral Organist in the country. Graham Elliott played a leading part in starting the North Wales Music Festival which is centred on St. Asaph Cathedral. He left St. Asaph Cathedral in 1981 on being appointed to Chelmsford Cathedral as Master of the Music.

In addition to his work with the Cathedral Choir he is the founder and Director of the Chelmsford Cathedral Festival. Dr. Elliott is a Professor at the Guildhall School of Music and broadcasts regularly on radio and television with the Cathedral Choir and as a soloist. Dr. Elliott's research interests are in the music of Benjamin Britten.

His academic qualifications are B.Mus. (University of Wales) 1970, M.A. 1982, Ph.D. (Wales) 1985, F.R.C.O., F.T.C.L., F.L.C.M., A.R.A.M. His hobbies are swimming, mediaeval architecture and English monasticism.

JOHN THEODORE BELCHER was born in Orpington, Kent, on 3rd December, 1937 and was educated at Tonbridge School. He studied at the Royal College of Music where he was a pupil of Sir John Dykes Bower and where he gained the Stewart Prize. He then proceeded to Trinity Hall, Cambridge, where he studied Music and History, and continued organ lessons with Sir David Willcocks, 1958-62.

While a student, he was Organist of Knockholt Parish Church, 1956-61 and on leaving University he became Organist of Holy Trinity Church, Folkestone, 1963-67 and conducted the Folkestone and Hythe Orchestral Society. In 1967 he was appointed Assistant Organist of Chester Cathedral, and he founded the Cantores Sine Nomine in Chester. Four years later he moved to Bournemouth as Organist of St. Peter's, the town's mother church, and taught piano and organ at Winchester College.

In 1981 he became Organist and Master of the Choristers at St. Asaph Cathedral and in addition was appointed Associate Conductor of the St. Asaph Choral Society. In 1985 he moved to Tewkesbury Abbey where he is currently Organist and Master of the Choristers.

He is M.A., F.R.C.O. 1962, (CHM) 1964, A.R.C.M. (Organ performing), and holds the Certificate in Education. His publications include 'The Organ – Holy Trinity, Folkestone' (1966), (British Institute of Organ Studies – BIOS – Vol 15 Nos 3 & 4 – October 1991), 'The Organs of Chester Cathedral' (1970) and 'The Organs of St. Peter's Church, Bournemouth' (1976).

He was Organ Adviser to the Diocese of Portsmouth from 1979 to 1981. He is an Examiner for the Associated Board of the Royal Schools of Music. His leisure pursuits include Architecture (especially Victorian churches) and swimming.

HUGH DAVIES was born in Fishguard in South Wales on 17th March, 1952. While at Fishguard Secondary School he studied with Peter Boorman at St. David's Cathedral. Afterwards he won a scholarship to St. Catharine's College, Cambridge and studied with Peter le Huray and Gillian Weir. He has the following qualifications: B.A. (1973), Mus.B. (1974), M.A. (1977), F.R.C.O. (1974).

In 1974, he was appointed Assistant Organist of Carlisle Cathedral, and during the following eleven years built up a fine reputation as a recitalist and choir trainer.

He was appointed Organist and Master of the Choristers at St. Asaph Cathedral in 1985, and has since continued to give recitals and play for broadcasts as well as maintaining a high standard of music in this very ancient Cathedral.

His leisure pursuits are reading and cooking, he is a member of the International Wine Society and he is also conductor of St. Asaph Choral Society.

THE ORGAN IN ST. ASAPH CATHEDRAL

The organ is first mentioned in the records in 1535 when £40 was paid for an instrument. This was replaced a hundred years later when a large organ, possibly by Robert Dallam, was erected.

There are a number of Orders of Chapter between 1675 and 1686 relating to repairs to the organ by a 'Mr Smith'. 'Mr Smith' was the famous organ builder Bernard Smith (formerly Schmidt) who came from Halle and built organs for Westminster Abbey, the Sheldonian Theatre, Oxford, Durham Cathedral, St. Paul's Cathedral, London and Trinity College, Cambridge. This organ served the Cathedral until it was sold in 1740.

It was replaced by an instrument of Abraham Jordan, a builder of great repute, and it cost the Cathedral authorities £447. A little over forty years later, however, the records tell that the Organist, John Jones, had his salary cut by £20 because there was no organ to play.

In 1834 William Hill built a one-manual organ. Additions were made throughout the nineteenth cenutry and it was rebuilt in 1897 when Hugh Percy Allen was Organist, and emerged as a four-manual organ with forty-two speaking stops. After seventy years of use, with only minor changes and restoration, the organ was completely rebuilt in 1966 with a new console, as a three-manual organ with forty-eight speaking stops.

MUSIC AT ST. ASAPH

by Hugh Davies

The last 6½ years has been a time of considerable development for the Cathedral Choir. After some successful recruiting campaigns for choristers, we have managed to maintain a steady improvement which has enabled us to tackle successfully a much wider repertoire and sing it to a high standard. As well as the busy round of weekday and Sunday services, the choir often takes part in concerts and has recently made a recording of Christmas music.

The present numbers (February 1992) stand at 17 choristers, 8 probationers and 15 senior and junior layclerks. The repertoire ranges from Tallis, Tye and Byrd through to Howells, Berkeley and Langlais.

The Cathedral Organists Association Conference was held at St. Asaph and Bangor Cathedrals in 1990.

ST. DAVID'S CATHEDRAL EGLWYS GADEIRIOL TŶ DDEWI

No cathedral settlement in Britain has a longer continuous story than St. David's. For more than fourteen centuries, there has been a Christian community in this pastoral valley at the westermost tip of Wales.

Much that is unique about modern St. David's stems from the choice of this place by David in the middle of the sixth century.

Text by H. Marriott from the Cathedral Guide Book.

ST. DAVID'S CATHEDRAL ORGANISTS

Herbert Charles Morris	1896-1922	Nicholas Jackson	1977-1984
Joseph Soar	1922-1953	Malcolm Gruffydd Watts	1984-1990
Peter Boorman	1953-1977	Kerry Jason Beaumont	1990

HERBERT CHARLES MORRIS was born on 18th June, 1873 in Coventry. He was educated at Coventry Grammar School and was a pupil of Frank Spinney at Leamington Spa and A. H. Brewer, Organist of St. Michael's Church, Coventry. During the years 1891-94 he was an Organ Exhibitioner at the Royal College of Music where he was a pupil of Sir Walter Parratt.

At some time he was pupil-assistant to Edwin Lemare at Holy Trinity, Sloane Street, London. Other early organ appointments were at Kenilworth Parish Church at various London churches and at Boscombe Pavilion. In 1895 he became Assistant Organist at Manchester Cathedral at the time when J. Kendrick Pyne was the Organist there. In 1896 he became Organist of St. Andrew's Church, Bath but within a short while took up his post at St. David's Cathedral. Later, while still Organist of St. David's Cathedral, he graduated at Downing College, Cambridge as M.A. having already gained the F.R.C.O., L.R.A.M., and A.R.C.M. diplomas.

He composed anthems, services and other church music, some of which was published. During the First World War he served in the RAF. He left St. David's Cathedral in 1921, not long after the disestablishment of the Church in Wales, whereupon he became Organist of Queen Street Congregational Church in Wolverhampton, staying there until his retirement in 1938. He died on 15th January, 1940.

It is interesting that not long after H. C. Morris had been appointed Organist of St. David's Cathedral, William Harris, the future Organist of St. George's Chapel, Windsor, became his pupil and assistant.

JOSEPH SOAR was born at Chapeltown, near Sheffield on 9th October, 1878. He was educated privately and at the Royal College of Music where he was an Exhibitioner, also he was a pupil-assistant to Dr. (later Sir) Walford Davies at the Temple Church.

At the age of 14 he had been Organist of the Parish Church, Chapeltown, now while training in London, he held Organists posts at St. John's Church, Clapham, then at All Saint's Church, Norfolk Square. In 1900 he took the F.R.C.O., becoming Organist of All Saint's Parish Church, Derby (later the Cathedral) during the following year. In 1904 he moved on to Barnsley Parish Church as Organist and in 1910, took the Durham degree of B.Mus. During this time also he was Conductor of the Tankersley Choral Society, Barnsley Amateur Operatic Society and the St. Cecilia Choral Society, Barnsley, 1904-1915, in addition to being Music Master at Barnsley Grammar School. In 1912 he became Organist of Halifax Parish Church but only until 1915, when he saw Military Service, first at Gallipoli, then at the Western Front of Egypt, and finally in India as Lieutenant IARO.

On resuming his career he became Organist of Burnham-on-Sea Parish Church in 1921, moving on to St. David's Cathedral in 1922. There he became a legendary figure for a variety of reasons. Soon he undertook an additional position which was most unusual for the Cathedral Organist, that of Coxswain of the St. David's lifeboat. If the harpoon went up during a service it was not unknown for him to leave the organ and make off for the lifeboat. In due course he became Hon. Secretary of the lifeboat station in 1926, and he received the bronze medallion for gallantry from the Royal National Lifeboat Institution in 1943. Meanwhile in 1934, he had received the Lambeth degree of D.Mus., and in 1936 had been President of the National Eisteddfod when it was held at Abergwaun (Fishguard). From 1933 until 1946 he was an Examiner and a Member of the Council of the Royal College of Organists, also during the Second World War years 1940-44 he was a Commandant in the Special Constabulary.

A man with such a diversity of interests obviously was a great character and good company. His old teacher, Walford Davies, who now had a cottage on the sand dunes outside St. David's, apparantly enjoyed visiting the Cathedral where "Joseph Soar played the organ when he was not captaining the lifeboat or sitting on the magisterial bench."*

Not surprisingly a variety of honours came his way. There was the MBE in 1947, Deputy Lieutenant for the County of Pembroke in 1950, Organist Emeritus when he retired from his work at the Cathedral in 1954, Hon. Life Governor, R.N.L.I. in 1960, and County President of the British Legion in Pembrokeshire. Despite such an active life Dr. Soar had still found time to compose some psalm chants, music for the Communion Service and some canticles for Evensong as well as some songs, part-songs and piano music. In retirement he lived close to Whitesands Bay, enjoying an occasional swim almost to the day of his death, 9th June, 1971, exactly four months short of his 94th birthday.

* H. C. Colles: Walford Davies – a biography (O.U.P. – 1942)

PETER BOORMAN was born on 6th February, 1923 at Walkern, Herts.

During the week of August 13th-17th, 1956, there was a festival in St. David's Cathedral to mark the tercentenary of the death of the famous composer, Thomas Tomkins, whose father was Organist of St. David's Cathedral. The programme included the unveiling of the Tomkins Memorial Organ case by Harry Gabb, Organist, Choirmaster and Composer at Her Majesty's Chapel Royal, who later gave an organ recital.

There was a lecture by Denis Stevens, Visiting Professor of Musicology at Columbia University, and a lecture recital by Thurston Dart, the world famous musicologist and harpsichordist. There were recitals by the famous viola gamba player Desmond Dupré, by the great counter-tenor Alfred Deller and his Deller Consort with the London Consort of Viols, also by the Elizabethan Madrigal Singers of University College, Aberystwyth, along with two performances of the play by Dorothy Sayers "The Zeal of Thy House". The Cathedral Choir also took part, singing the Opening Service and in one of the concerts.

While Organist of St. David's Cathedral, Peter Boorman built up a fine series of organ recitals on Tuesday evenings during the summer in the Cathedral. Always he would produce the programmes himself beautifully set out and printed on his own hand printing press. Among the many notable organists to play at St. David's was the Vatican Organist, Fernando Germani.

In 1970 he appeared on BBC 2 TV in a programme Organ Organ. A write up in the Radio Times, 26th February, 1970 showed him to be a multi-talented man, amateur printer, experimental vintner, linguist (he had learnt Welsh) and teacher.

NICHOLAS JACKSON is the grandson of the noted architect Sir Thomas Graham Jackson. He succeeded to the family baronetcy (Fane St. George) in 1979. Born on 4th September, 1933, he was educated firstly at Radley College then at Wadham College, Oxford and finally at the Royal Academy of Music (1956-59) where he studied the organ with C. H. Trevor. Afterwards he went to Holland to study the harpsichord with Gustav Leonhardt and at some time he was also a pupil of George Malcolm. He holds the L.R.A.M. and A.R.C.M. diplomas.

He was Organist of the London churches of St. Anne's, Soho, (1963–68); St. James' Church, Piccadilly, (1971-74); St. Lawrence, Jewry–next Guildhall, (1974-77). Next he became Organist and Master of the Choristers at St. David's Cathedral in 1977, and not long afterwards set about founding the St. David's Cathedral Bach Festival, which he directed and which has become one of the leading musical events in Wales.

Already before going to St. David's he had been directing his own chamber orchestra which gave annual concerts at the Queen Elizabeth Hall and such venues as the Victoria and Albert Museum and the Whitehall Banqueting Hall. On his return to London therefore, in 1984, he developed further his work with his Concertante of London, whose 15 to 20 members also play in the London Symphony Orchestra and other such notable orchestras, taking them all over Spain to Lograno, to Malaga, Santiago de Compostela, Valencia and to Llivia. In addition he became director of the Festival-Bach at the monastry in Santes Creus, furthermore he took a section of the orchestra to play in the Ciudadela Festival (1987). He has developed the orchestra still further by absorbing into it the London Gabrieli Brass Ensemble and, for the performance of J. S. Bach cantatas, a choir.

Nicholas Jackson is recognised as being one of the most outstanding organists and harpsichordists in England. He made his debut as a harpsichordist at the Wigmore Hall (1963), and is frequently invited to give concerts in both Europe and the U.S.A. having given performances at the Royal Festival Hall and the Queen Elizabeth Hall in London; in Notre Dame, Paris; Chartres Cathedral; in Berlin and in New York; also in the Teatro Real, Madrid; the Santa Eulalia in Palma de Mallorca and in Granada. He has given several organ concerts in Mahon (1978, 1985) and, more recently, in 1990, he gave the first festival concert at the Santa Maria Church.

As a solo harpsichordist he has played with a number of different orchestras and on one occasion, at the Queen Elizabeth Hall, played the five harpsichord concertos of J. S. Bach.

He has made more than 20 recordings of works for the organ and for the harpsichord, including some of his own compositions. He has also made a casette recording entitled "The Music of Spain", on the baroque organ of the Santes Creus Monastery, near Tarragona, and another with Maurice Murphy, principal trumpet of the London Symphony Orchestra.

In addition he has made three recordings in the USA for a series entitled "The Art of the Harpsichordist".

He has recorded most of his own music including "Mass for a Saint's Day" which was composed in 1966, and recorded in 1971. In addition he has composed and published a "Twentieth Century Merbecke", 1967; "Four Images" for organ, 1971; a "Solemn Mass", 1977; an "Organ Sonata" and a "Suite for Brass Quintet and Organ" which is also playable in a version for trumpet and organ.

He is in the process of composing an Opera called "The Reluctant Highwayman" which is based on the real life story of an 18th Century rake who was born well, educated at Eton College and finally was hanged at Tyburn. He is also making a Compact Disc for Priory Records at Segovia Cathedral in April 1992.

MALCOLM GRUFFYDD WATTS was born on 6th May, 1947 at Cardigan, Wales. He was educated at Cardigan and at Cardiff University and was awarded a B.Mus. (Honours) degree in 1968 and he also gained a Diploma in Education.

He studied the organ with Robert Joyce at Llandaff Cathedral during his years at Cardiff. He became the Head of Music at schools in Port Talbot, Haverfordwest and Whitland and he was appointed Assistant Organist of St. David's Cathedral in 1977.

He was acting-organist from September, 1984 and was appointed fully to the post of Organist and Choirmaster on 1st November, 1984. He left on 31st August, 1990.

He was Artistic Director of the Cathedral Bach Festival and in his first Bach Festival he gave the organ recital which included the first performance of a commissioned work, "Passacaglia" by Hoddinott. He also gave the first performance of Parrott's 2nd Suite for Organ in a summer recital (1986).

Under his direction the trebles of the choir gave the first performance of evening services by Parrott and Seimion Morris, and the full choir of a work by David Nevens "Adeste Sancta Trinitas". He extended the repertoire and number of services to include Evensong on Tuesday with a small choir, trebles on Wednesday and full choral services on Sunday at 11am and 6pm. He continued the membership of the R.S.C.M., and trained girls successfully for the St. Cecilia Junior Award.

He introduced a system of bursaries for choristers who were successful in instrumental examinations. The choir sang a large number of settings and anthems, and a treble line comprising mainly girls, was a new venture from 1984.

The choir took part in many special services, funerals, weddings, consecrations of bishops and archbishops, parts of which were televised. The choir gave recitals in the Cathedral and other venues, e.g., St. Mary's, Tenby, Nevern, Aberystwyth, Llanelli, Llandeilo and Carmarthen. Malcolm Watts considered the choral tradition at St. David's Cathedral to be of great importance.

With regard to the organ itself, Malcolm Watts arranged to have a number of much needed additions and these included the addition of a mixture stop on the Swell and Great, a new open metal 16′ for the pedals and a new (acquired second-hand) full length 32′ open wood to the pedals.

These added new dimensions in sound to the instrument, but Mr Watts considers that more needs to be done.

KERRY JASON BEAUMONT was born on 5th April, 1957 in Cambridge. He was educated at Ripon Cathedral Choir School and at St. Michael's Cathedral Choir School, Toronto (R.C.). He gained the B.Mus. Degree in Organ Performance at the Curtis Institute of Music, Philadelphia. He gained another diploma whilst still in Canada, the A.R.C.T. (Associate of the Royal Conservatory of Toronto) in Piano Performance and in Organ Performance. British diplomas that he gained are:- F.R.C.O. (CHM), F.T.C.L. in Organ Performance, L.R.A.M. in Organ Teaching, A.R.C.M. in Organ Performance. He received an M.A. degree in 20th Century Music and Composition from Durham University in 1991.

Mr Beaumont's Organ Teachers were Ronald Perrin – Organist of Ripon Cathedral, Peter Daly of Toronto, John Weaver of Philadelphia, Antoine Reboulot in Quebec for organ improvisation and literature, and Pierre Cochereau in France for organ improvisation.

He has gained several prizes for organ, including the Limpus Prize in the A.R.C.O. examination, 1989, the Young Artists (First Prize) Philadelphia Chapter; American Guild of

Organists, 1875, the International Organ Improvisation Competition, San Anselmo, California, 1986 (First Prize) and the Coventry Cathedral Recital Award in 1989 for the F.R.C.O. examination playing.

His previous posts:- 1973-75, Organ Scholar, St. Michael's Cathedral, Toronto, 1981-88, Organist/Music Director, Church of the Good Samaritan (Episcopal) Paoli, Pennsylvania, USA, 1988-89, Lay Clerk/Ripon Cathedral, 1990, Music Teacher/Repton School, Derbyshire. He was appointed Organist and Master of the Choristers at St. David's Cathedral in 1990.

His recordings:- Direct-To-Tape Recording Co., New Jersey, USA, 'Seasons of Improvisations' one being released in 1991, Cantoris Records (Lincoln) 'The Organ of St. David's Cathedral'.

His broadcasts:- National Public Radio, USA (Improvisations), National Radio, Holland (Improvisations). Mr Beaumont gave concerts in Canada, USA and UK. He is married with two children.

MUSIC AT ST. DAVID'S – 1990/91

by Kerry J. Beaumont, Organist and Master of the Choristers

In June 1991 the choirs of St. David's Cathedral increased the number of Choral Evensong Services to four or five evenings per week during school term time. In April 1991 the trebles of the Cathedral Choir were separated and augmented to form two choirs: a Girls Choir (ages 8 to 18) and a new Cathedral Boys Choir (ages 8 to 13). In May 1991 a small chamber choir of adults (The Chapel Choir) was founded.

In June 1991 the Cathedral Choir (Girls and Lay Clerks) sang Haydn's Missa Brevis Sanctii Joannis de Deo with the London Festival Orchestra as part of the British Gas Cathedral Classics concerts series. In July 1991 the trebles (Girls Choir and some of the Boys Choir) sang in a performance of Britten's St. Nicolas for a Fishguard Festival concert which was later broadcast on BBC Radio 3 and in August 1991 the Cathedral Choir appeared on BBC 2 Television as part of the series 'Titmarsh's Travels', a documentary about places of pilgrimage in the UK.

THE ORGAN OF ST. DAVID'S CATHEDRAL

There is evidence that an organ existed in St. David's Cathedral as early as 1490 when Walter Warryn was paid 40 shillings for playing the organ. Further reference was made in 1565 "for making two stops for ye great Organs", the cost being 6d. In 1581, an order was made for a new organ to be made "ad usum divini servitii" by the Bishop. All that is known about this instrument is that it was situated under the western arch of the tower on the rood screen.

John West in his book 'Cathedral Organists Past and Present', tells the following story. The following incident concerning the Organist of St. David's, at the time of the attack upon the Cathedral by the Parliamentary troops during the Civil Wars, is worth quoting:

"The rebels were consulting in the Choir about what other sacrilegious mischiefs they should perform; it was at length agreed to destroy the organ. The Organist, who had secreted himself within the organ loft, heard the same, and knowing that, if they perpetrated their intended mischief, he should lose his bread, he threw a large stone into the Choir; which falling on the head of one of Cromwell's aides-de-camp killed him.

Dreading the consequence of his being discovered and taken by the rebels, he fled; they perceived, and pursued him, when he had the presence of mind to get into one of the bells which hung low, and there he supported himself by the clapper, until they had given up the search." – 'History and Antiquities of the Parish of St. David's', by Captain Geo. W. Manby, R.N.

It was decided on the 26th July, 1698 "to provide an organ with all convenient speed" by the Chantor and Chapter. The work was entrusted to the celebrated Bernard Schmidt (better known as "Father Smith"). The cost of the organ was £290.

This organ stood on the rood screen and had casework made of Norwegian oak supposedly carved by Grinling Gibbons. This organ had one manual and no pedals. The organ was rebuilt, resited and enlarged in 1843 by Lincoln.

Between the years 1865 and 1883 the Cathedral was being restored by George Gilbert Scott and the organ was not in use. At the end of this period the decision was taken that a new organ should be built and 'Father' Henry Willis was contracted to do the work.

In 1900 Vincent Willis added the Pedal Trombone. The organ was rebuilt in 1906 but no details survive as to what was done or who carried out the work. Alterations were made in 1920-21, but again no details survive.

In 1934 Henry Willis III proposed some triforium additions to aid congregational singing in the nave. This idea was never acted upon at St. David's.

On September 7th, 1945, Joseph Soar requested that the Dean should contact Messrs. Willis and Sons over the bad condition of the organ blower. At this time the required wind pressure was produced using water power, there being no electricity at the Cathedral. The organ in the Tabernacle Chapel was powered by the same water supply as the Cathedral and stories were told that when the Cathedral organ was being played the Chapel organ was badly short of wind.

In 1953 Hill, Norman and Beard undertook a major rebuild of the organ. A new case was built by Alban Caroe, which replaced the original construction of pipe racks. At the same time a new console and electro-pneumatic action was provided.

In 1966 a 32′ reed was added to the Pedal division. Twenty pipes were borrowed from the Trombone, the bottom octave being electronic. In 1980 Rushworth and Dreaper restored the organ, recasting the enclosed Choir organ with a Positive-type chorus.

In 1986, mixtures were added to the Swell and Great by Percy Daniel and Sons. At the same time the Pedal Octave was replaced by metal pipes having previously been made of wood. In 1989 a 32′ Open Wood was installed to the Pedal organ. An Open Metal rank of pipes was also added to the Pedal organ giving a very definite 16′ tone. Storm damage at the end of 1990 necessitated the repair of the Pedal Trombone and Choral Bass.

Two trumpeting angels are a happy modern addition to the organ projection of the parapet over the choir entrance.

In 1976, a two manual organ was installed in the Lady Chapel. It was built by S. E. Gilks of Peterborough.